The Energy of Belief

*Psychology's Power Tools
To Focus Intention and Release
Blocking Beliefs*

Sheila Sidney Bender, PhD
and
Mary T. Sise, LCSW

Energy Psychology Press
Santa Rosa, California

The Energy of Belief

Library of Congress Cataloging-in-Publication Data

Bender, Sheila S.
  The energy of belief: psychology's power tools to focus intention and release blocking beliefs / Sheila Sidney Bender and Mary T. Sise. — 1st ed.
    p. cm.
  Includes bibliographical references and index.
  ISBN: 978-1-60415-019-3 (pbk. : alk. paper)
  1. Energy psychology. I. Sise, Mary T. II. Title.
  RC489.E53B46 2007
  616.89'1—dc22
                            2007034486

Typeset in Cochin

Printed in USA

First Edition

Typeset by Karin Kinsey

Cover design by Victoria Valentine

10 9 8 7 6 5 4 3 2

To the memory of my parents, Claire and Jack Sidney,

With love,

—Sheila Sidney Bender

To my husband, Jack,

With love and gratitude for your constant love and support.

—Mary T. Sise

Acknowledgments

The *Energy of Belief* could not have been written without the help of colleagues, patients, friends, neighbors, and family. They span not only the United States, but throughout the world. Their energy, their interest, and their contributions whether with a good word, a conversation about a new clinical strategy, or with hours of reading and editing the manuscript, allowed us to write this book.

Together we thank our editors Dara Monahan, Roberta Lawrence, Faith Teeple, Courtney Arnold, and our publisher Dawson Church; our readers Claire Sidney, Jeannette Hoffman, Barbara Holstein, Elliot Bender, MaryGrace Lattig, Margaret Fontana, Meghan Sise, Katie Sweeney, MaryAnn Morrison, and Jan Willard; our photographers Scott Kahn, MaryEllen Morrow, Anthony Prizzi, Joseph Bender, Tracy Caldwell, and Alden Ford; and our illustrators John H. Diepold Sr. and Molly Cobb. We thank our photography models Andrew Portuguese, Thachana Heron, Dwight "Juice" Jones, Tiffany Antonenko, Sebastian DeSalvo, Julia Diepold, Mark Snyder, Michael Bender, Joseph Bender, Katie Sweeney, Meghan Sise, and John H. Diepold Jr.

for their patience and cooperation during the shooting sessions. We are thankful for the contributions of John H. Diepold Jr., Victoria Britt, Steve Steinberg, Teri Steinberg, Phil Friedman, Richard Shapiro, and Jane Tucker and the assistance of Janet Kaczmarek, Elissa Teeple, Misti Galvez, Rhonda the postal employee in Oakland, California, and James, the concierge at the Hilton Hawaiian Village.

Although the following are separate lists, we each add our appreciation to the other's personal circle.

Bender Personal Acknowledgments

I thank Victoria Britt and John H. Diepold Jr. for their help in making our professional book available to you. Thank you, John, for touch-and-breathe, elaters, and the use of your dad's beautiful illustration of the hand. Thank you, Victoria, for your story of Jeremy and Julia and being there behind the scenes. I want to thank my mother, Claire Sidney, for being a great reader and helping me get the book started. I think had she lived to see the book's completion, she would have increased our sales tremendously by giving one to her friends and any one else she met along the way. I miss you, mom.

Much gratitude to dear friends who listened to my one topic of conversation for the past year and were so encouraging. Thank you to Jeannette Hoffman, MaryGrace Lattig, MaryEllen Morrow, Edith Leonardis, Dawn Gemeinhardt and Mia.

Most of all I want to thank my sons Michael and Joseph for their incredible resilience. They learned to find new ways to eat when the cupboards were bare. Thank you to those who took them in and fed them when they pressed their noses against a friend's window. My gratitude to the Portuguese, Shapiro, Cappabianca, Sainato, and Bollettieri families.

Sise Personal Acknowledgments

This book would not be written without the help of many people. I would like to thank the thousands of clients who allowed me to use these "new energy techniques" with them, long before we were ever aware of how effective they would be. I am especially grateful for the clients from whom the stories in this book are drawn. Your courage and strength inspire me every day.

I am also very thankful for my family: my husband Jack, my children Meghan, Jack, and Katie, and Brian Sweeney for their continued patience with me as I spent another day in front of my computer, or another weekend at a conference teaching and learning about energy psychology. I am grateful for my parents: Ray and Theresa Ebert, for encouraging me to be all that I can be, and to pursue my dreams, no matter what others believed. I drew from this foundation each time I was confronted by someone who challenged my supporting this new field of psychotherapy. I am grateful to my siblings: Ray, Jerry, John, Joan, Jim, Judy, Julie, JoAnn, Katie, Ed and Matt for the role each one of them played in my own personal growth.

I want to thank Roger Callahan for developing and teaching me Thought Field Therapy. It revolutionized my clinical practice, and opened up for me the door to the energy psychology world. His discoveries have enabled me to train hundreds of clinicians and successfully help hundreds of patients.

Thank you to my wonderful local energy psychology colleagues for all of their challenging ideas, wisdom, and support including: Betsy Osborne, Margie Wood, Maureen Sullivan, Terry Reinhardt, Suzanne Tombs, Emily Gallagher, Mary Daignault, Frank Macri, Jim Grinter, Martin Pearlman, Cindy Taylor, Danielle Stokley, Lorrie Golden, Deb Nozik, and Nita Rowinski.

Having been in the energy psychology world for over a decade there have been numerous international colleagues whose work inspired my own. Through the Association for Comprehensive

Energy Psychology (ACEP) Conferences and worldwide e-mail lists, their generosity in sharing practice wisdom in a collegial and open spirit will never be forgotten. In particular I would like to thank: David Feinstein, Donna Eden, David Gruder, Fred Gallo, Vicki Matthews, Gloria Arenson, Carol Look, Pat Carrington, Suzanne Connelly, Dorothea Hover-Kramer, Paula Shaw, Debby Vadja, Norma Feldman, Ron Ruden, Larry Stoler, Carol Stern, Greg Nicosia, Maria Becker, Mary Hammond, Mary Jo Bulbrook, Bob Schwarz, John Freedom, Loretta Sparks, Sharon Toole, Gary Craig, Tapas Fleming, Asha Clinton, Judith Swack, Don Elium, Larry Nims, Andy Hahn, Lynn Karjala, Steve Reed, Nan Lu, Maggie Phillips, Sandi Radomski, Michael Galvin, John Hartung, Jim Klopman, Mary Clark, Barb Stone, Dawson Church, Ann Adams, Phil Friedman, Gary Peterson, and Jim Kowal.

My work in the understanding and treatment of trauma has also been blessed with many gifted teachers, especially Bessel van der Kolk, Belleruth Naparstek, Bill O'Hanlon, Bob Scaer, Karen Kovacic, and Peter Levine. Thank you.

Lastly, I am very grateful to the writings of the Saint Germain Foundation and also the teachings of Her Holiness Sai Maa Lakshmi Devi for making me aware of the immense power behind the words "I AM." Understanding the importance of those two words, caused me to change my therapy practice and focus in a deeper and more profound way with clients on their beliefs. I am honored to be able to bring to the general public a way to incorporate this knowledge with the powerful, transformational healing modality of Touch and Breathe (TAB).

Contents

Introduction

Have you ever been frustrated by an unwanted thought that keeps rolling around in your mind and you can't stop thinking about it? Have you ever wondered why you are afraid to do something before you even attempt it? Are you sometimes surprised by your strong angry overreaction to someone you love, only to feel guilty and ashamed afterward? Have you tried talking about it until you are absolutely sick of listening to yourself? Are you just tired of responding in the same unproductive ways despite your best intentions?

We, a psychologist and clinical social worker, also wanted to know why negative beliefs, thoughts and behaviors continued as if they had a life of their own, and why talking about the problem and other traditional therapeutic attempts to eliminate the problem were not enough. We wanted to learn ways to help our patients regain control of their lives. In our search for the answers, we have been fortunate to be part of a professional movement that has laid the groundwork for a new branch of psychology called energy psychology. This is our invitation to you to learn and use an energy psychology method that we call Touch and Breathe (TAB).

You, the Reader

It is likely that you are reading this because you have a problem with a self-defeating or self-sabotaging belief, thought, or behavior and want to try something on your own. Your problem may be a specific fear or phobia. It may be a thought that you can't get out of your head or a behavior or unhealthy habit that you are unable to stop. It could be as serious as drug addiction, or as benign as video game playing, or a habit of procrastination that ultimately gets in the way of a more productive lifestyle. You may simply be sick and tired of repeated irrational negative beliefs about yourself.

While searching for a solution for your problem perhaps you may have already heard about energy psychology. Many people who have been to a chiropractor or acupuncturist have been exposed to and have become acquainted with some core concepts of energy psychology. Other people may have had experiences with practices such as yoga, meditation, and Reiki, and some readers may have discovered books on energy psychology methods and are familiar with energy tapping. On the other hand, you may know absolutely nothing about energy psychology but are curious enough to learn about it. No matter where on this spectrum you find yourself, you are in the right place to make a meaningful change in your life.

Why This Self-Help Book?

The Energy of Belief came as a direct response to the requests that the meridian-based treatment described in a textbook written for professionals about the same issues *(Diepold, Britt & Bender, 2004)* should also be developed for self-treatment. In this book you will find much of what was taught in the professional one, but in ways that help you self-apply the concepts and techniques to overcome your problem thoughts, beliefs, and behaviors.

Author and Psychologist, Sheila Bender Writes

I have been fortunate to have a long-standing association and friendship with three colleagues, psychologist John H. Diepold Jr., and social workers Victoria Britt and Mary Sise. John, Victoria and I formed the BDB Group (Britt, Diepold, Bender) and studied, taught, and wrote about our clinical experiences. In March 2004, we published a textbook on the therapy entitled *Evolving Thought Field Therapy: The Clinician's Handbook of Diagnoses, Treatment, and Theory,* which describes evolving thought field therapy (EvTFT), a meridian-based method of energy psychology.

Although written for professionals, nonclinicians expressed interest in the book because they wanted to know more about energy psychology in general and EvTFT in particular. Our patients wanted to use the book as a guide to at-home work while nonpatients, having some familiarity with other meridian-based therapies like thought field therapy (TFT) and emotional freedom techniques (EFT), were curious about the differences and similarities among them. The technique of touch-and-breathe (TAB) that John (Diepold, 1998, 2000) developed in lieu of tapping to achieve the treatment effects was especially intriguing because of its gentleness and promotion of mindfulness.

Unfortunately, most lay readers found our book too technical, and requested that we write something that a nonprofessional could use. In order to write such a book, I invited Mary to join me because I knew she had a gift for teaching difficult information in an easy-to-understand way.

Author and Social Worker, Mary Sise Writes

I was thrilled when Sheila asked me to collaborate with her on this book. As the past president of the Association for Comprehensive Energy Psychology (ACEP), I had spent countless hours integrating energy psychology into the mental health field. My primary focus was to make these methods available not only to my own patients but to other therapists as well through the course work and videos I had developed for professionals who treated trauma and post-traumatic stress disorder (PTSD). Having used energy psychology methods for over ten years and witnessing their incredible success, especially in releasing traumatic experiences, I also began to recognize the importance of using energy psychology methods for clients' beliefs. I was constantly amazed at how powerful negative beliefs were, not only to stop someone from reaching a specific goal, but also how they seemed to play out as a life theme. I learned quickly that treatments and therapy that worked only to change a current situation or symptom would fail, as the energy of these negative beliefs resurfaced again and again in different situations and scenarios until they were dealt with once and for all. I am tremendously grateful to have the opportunity to bring this energy psychology method to the general public, especially in relation to the energy of beliefs.

How to Use This Book

In the first half of this book you will learn to use a meridian-based *algorithm*, which is a set of uniform steps everyone will use. In later chapters you will be taught ways to go deeper to understand emotions and beliefs that may be lurking below your current level of awareness and apply methods that tailor self-treatment according to your unique needs. In addition, we have created a video to demonstrate the actual treatment steps at www.energyofbelief.com.

The book is not designed to replace medical and psychotherapeutic treatment when needed in addition to or separate from the self-help techniques. In addition, there are helpful resources listed at the back of this book, including how to locate an energy psychology practitioner in your area.

Overall Structure of Book

There are twelve chapters and they are designed to build on one another. You will learn new techniques in each chapter, so it is a good idea to do the practice exercises as you come to them in each chapter before moving on to the next one. Also, each chapter begins with an introduction to what you will learn and its importance. Using the illustrations, pictures, diagrams and verbal directions you will go step by step through each of the procedures. The first five chapters will teach you the basics of TAB and in Chapters Six through Ten you will learn more about your energy system to further personalize your self-work. Chapter 11 will provide a guide to future performance and the final chapter is a look at how the healing work you do for yourself impacts the world.

Chapter One:
Master Your Energy to Transform Your Life

This chapter is an introduction to your mind and the problems created by attempts to artificially separate what will be called **the physical you** and **the energy you.** You will learn about the energy of thoughts and a special kind of thought known as a belief. You will also learn about energy disruptions that act as walls and keep you from getting through to your goals and also the beliefs that keep walls in place. You will learn why neither your own pep talks nor advice given by friends and professionals may be enough to give you the necessary motivation to change, and why at times positive thinking isn't enough.

Chapter Two:
Understanding What is in Your Thought Fields

In this chapter we teach you about blocking beliefs and triggers, as well as the energetic signals in your thought fields that are theorized to be the source of the emotions that you feel when you think about a problem. You will learn how the energetic signal is not necessary to the thought field, and that when the signal is removed, you are better able to think about the problem and consider your options because you are no longer acting reflexively.

Chapter Three: The Components of TAB

This chapter is about the importance of meridians, mindfulness, touch, breath, intuition, and intention, and their synergy in TAB. Each of the terms is described in connection to TAB.

Chapter Four: The Steps of Basic TAB

This chapter acquaints you with the basic procedural steps for TAB; and the meridian treatment points, integration sequence and eye-roll are all described. You will learn how affirmations are useful as a source of energy for some of the exercises and the differences in TAB between statements of intention and affirmations.

Chapter Five: Basic TAB Practice

In this chapter you will take a problem you want to work on and we guide you through the TAB procedure.

Chapter Six:
Self-Communication: Using your Energy Feedback System

In this chapter you will learn about aspects of applied kinesiology relevant to TAB and how to self-test as a means of communicating between **the physical you** and **the energy you.**

Chapter Seven:
Polarity Disruptions and Neurological Disorganization

This chapter explains how to self-test for polarity disruptions and neurological disorganization, two key energy factors relevant for your successful self-work using TAB. You will learn how these energy factors may account for why logic alone sometimes is not enough.

Chapter Eight: The Energetic Impact of Beliefs on Your Intentions

In this chapter you will be exploring more about how your thoughts and beliefs have energy. You will learn the necessary steps to take to identify when there is a blocking belief that is impacting your current intention to solve a problem, and strategies to release it.

Chapter Nine: The Energetic Impact of Core Beliefs

This chapter describes the impact of your core beliefs and teaches you a way to use TAB to replace any negative belief that you have with a healthier belief.

Chapter Ten: Personalized TAB to Increase Intuition & Self-Awareness

In this chapter, through illustrations, pictures, diagrams and verbal directions you will learn the focus areas associated with the meridian treatment points you've already used in Chapters Four and Five. You will also learn some of the emotions associated with these areas to further your self-awareness and identify personal treatment points.

Chapter Eleven: Creating the Life You Want

This is a chapter about developing your future through your thoughts, beliefs, and intentions. You will learn to imagine and rehearse the life you want in your mind and integrate those strategies with TAB treatments. You will see how this technique solidifies your goals and dreams, and makes them easier to achieve.

Chapter Twelve: World Peace Begins with Inner Peace

The emphasis in this chapter is on ways your individual inner energetic harmony impacts the world.

Your Invitation to Read On

We invite you to learn and use TAB to help you gain a foothold when slipping into the discomfort of unwanted thoughts and behaviors.

We also invite you to use TAB to offset the pleasures involved in self-destructive and compulsive behaviors such as nonstop eating, cigarette smoking, hair pulling, procrastination, and unhealthy love attractions. We invite you to look deeper when you are upset, and become increasingly aware of what is really troubling you. We invite you to investigate the beliefs or conclusions that you came to as a child that may no longer serve you. Once you are aware of these old patterns and thoughts, we invite you then to release these unhealthy beliefs or emotions so that you can live more fully in present time rather than in the past.

And finally, we invite you to envision the life you were meant to live. We want you to imagine what you would like to be, do, or have and, coupled with the TAB treatments, bring that idea into your energy field so you can fully resonate with it.

Our wish is that you use this powerful method to release your limiting beliefs and focus your energy to enrich your life and achieve your goals.

Now, let's begin.

All the Best,

Sheila & Mary

CHAPTER 1

Master Your Energy to Transform Your Life

For thousands of years ancient wisdom has recognized life energy within and around living human beings. It is known as *chi* in China, *prana* in India, *ki* in Japan, *nishama* in the Jewish tradition, and the *state of grace* in Christianity.

In the East, life energy became ingrained in the culture and is integral to the thinking about health and the treatment of illness. Mind, body, and spirit are inseparable. In both China and India, treatments and practices developed around life energy that included the pathways and areas for energy flow as well as descriptions of the patterns of this flow. In China, life energy, or chi, is described as flowing through channels that form a system known as the acupuncture meridian system. In India, life energy or *prana* flows through a system of energy centers known as chakras.

In this chapter, you will learn how the Western public was introduced to the concepts of life energy in Eastern medicine in the 1970s. We discuss how this information was integrated with traditional Western thinking, which provided the impetus for some innovative practices in both medicine and psychotherapy.

We also give you an introduction to your mind-body-energy system and discuss your life problems in terms of restrictions to the energy flow. Using the metaphor of walls, we discuss how your energy can become blocked in a way that, even with your best intentions, you are unable to reach your new goals.

We will give case examples of the walls that perhaps originally were built by your mind for protection but are now destructive and life-limiting. You will also find an overview about the energy of your thoughts and why working on energy, dammed up as walls, can free you to refocus that energy and create new options for yourself.

The chapter also introduces the central themes of *The Energy of Belief*:

1. Your mind is more than just your brain.

2. Your thoughts, emotions, and beliefs not only have energy, they are energy.

3. You can do self-work on the negative energetic aspects of your thoughts, emotions, and beliefs using an energy psychology technique called Touch and Breathe (TAB).

4. In TAB you use the acupuncture meridian system as a gateway to your mind-body-energy system.

5. Using TAB is effective because it releases the energy of the negative beliefs that block you from your goals and then uses the freed energy to help focus your intention to reach them.

Walls

What are walls? *Walls* are forces that keep you from achieving your goals. We've all hit walls or come up against walls. A wall might be an anger you can't let go of...a fear you can't shake...a job you're afraid to tackle...an old memory that intrudes and won't go away...or an unwanted behavior you struggle to stop. Walls may be connected to unpleasant emotions like hopelessness, helplessness and thoughts such as *what's the use?* Walls are kept in place by the negative beliefs you have about yourself, or the world in which you live. Beliefs, whether negative or positive, are thoughts that act as filters for your experiences and may be compared to tinted glasses that influence the color of all you see. Beliefs not only influence all you perceive and respond to in the outside world, they also affect how you view yourself. For example, if you have the belief "I deserve good things" you stand tall and reach for a far-off possibility, but if your belief is "I don't deserve good things," the energy of that belief keeps even the closest of opportunities out of reach.

Walls can begin by chance or develop over time as a means of protection. They are formed from your energy and require a continual supply of your energy to be kept in place. Sometimes the walls have a payoff; what you do to protect yourself works for a while. Even if it only works briefly, at least it is a small relief from feeling bad and it might even feel good for the moment. The problem is that the protection of a wall comes with a heavy price; it is difficult to seize a new opportunity when it means letting go of an old protection.

Walls of Protection

Walls of protection are those seemingly unexplained responses, such as feeling incredibly uncomfortable when paid a compliment, or feeling abject terror when your job requires you to travel. They are often accompanied by a belief such as "I am unsafe" and even though you may or may not remember how the wall got started, it doesn't matter.

Sally's Story

Sally, a 26-year-old software designer, described how she experienced a wall during another failed job interview despite her excellent credentials. "I go into an interview feeling fine. When I sit down and I see the interviewer, I suddenly feel as though I've crashed into something. I begin to think I am unsafe. I get a rush of thoughts and I think the person is picking my brain. This makes me terribly uncomfortable. I try not to signal my distress, so I don't speak; I clam up.

Afterward, I'm angry with myself for having such crazy thoughts and then I feel even worse. I know the thought is in my head, but I can't control my reactions."

Sally's wall began as a means of defense against a painful experience in her youth and grew into an insurmountable obstacle whenever she had a job interview. We shall continue to discuss her experience and her self-treatment later in the chapter.

Roman's Story

Roman, a 45-year-old financial banker, is fearless in his pursuit of deals, but was frightened in his search for a significant other. He described his wall, "I have a great job, a great car, and a great apartment, but my social life is nonexistent, a big zero. When I see someone I'd like to meet I suddenly act differently as I begin the social exchange. It's like a glass wall. I can't see it and I come crashing against it each time I try. I want the closeness but I just can't get there."

Although Roman had some guesses about why his wall existed, he did not remember any specific event or any particular belief related to it. Fortunately, it isn't necessary to know exactly what caused the problem, or when and where it began, for TAB to be effective. In TAB we focus on correcting the energy disturbances associated with thinking about the problem and releasing the blocking beliefs behind it. After working with TAB, Roman attended a friend's wedding and was sitting at the same table as a woman he found very interesting. Unlike many times before when the wall would keep him from engaging in conversation, Roman found talking to her easy despite the loud music. In fact, it was so easy he found himself smiling and relaxing during the course of the evening. Previously, he had not normally smiled when talking with a woman who interested him and as Roman later recalled, it was in that moment he knew he had passed the wall.

Both Sally and Roman responded to uncomfortable situations with immediate responses that were like knee-jerk reflexes that happened without a second thought. Although the beliefs that caused them to build these walls may have been valuable earlier in their lives, they are no longer useful now. As you can see, for Sally and

Roman, their former beliefs limited their ability to go after things they truly desired.

Joe's Story

Joe, a 38-year-old fireman, had a mild, chronic cough and was recently diagnosed with early-stage emphysema. Joe had smoked for over 20 years. He described his wall of frustration as he faced his doctor who told him, for the fifth time, that he needed to stop smoking. "I said to myself, 'Joe, just do it,' but I couldn't. It's like I had a wall in front of me, a very big wall. Believe me," Joe continued, "I've climbed tall ladders up high walls, but there's no ladder tall enough to get me over this one."

And then he added, "But you know, smoking makes me feel good. I don't want to believe that I am going to die if I keep smoking. I want to keep that thought out of my head."

Joe was so drawn to the good feelings while smoking that he didn't want to think of his deteriorating health, nor the concerns of his family who love him and want him to stop smoking.

Teresa's Story

Teresa is a marketing executive and single mother of two young children, who dragged through her day because she was so exhausted. Her job was in jeopardy but she couldn't seem to control a behavior she developed at home at the end of the day. Teresa explained, "I found that after a long day of work and when the kids were finally asleep I enjoyed playing FreeCell, Solitaire, or shopping on the Internet. It is extremely relaxing." Then with an edge to her voice she continued, "I crave time for myself when no one is asking me for anything, so being on the computer doing mindless things for hours seems like a perfect solution, except that it is way out of control. I am suddenly aware that it is two o'clock in the morning and I'm still saying 'just one more game.' It is as if while playing I am in a trance walled off from feeling."

Like Joe, Teresa had an *enjoyable* experience each time she played a computer game that was, in a sense, a time-out from the overwhelming family and job responsibilities she faced everyday. She described the experience as "feels numb, a good numb." Unfortunately, she re-experienced tension when a game was over, so she sought relief in the next game and the next game. People who get trapped in nonproductive and ultimately self-sabotaging activities keep doing it because it momentarily seems to relieve their tension, even though they realize that it is self-defeating in the end. In other words, you pursue a self-defeating action because you like it, because it helps you to feel good for the moment, and because it keeps reinforcing itself.

If walls are blocked energy, where do you find them? Joe, Roman, Sally, and Teresa didn't have the answer when asked to explain their location, and scientists don't either.

Where are Your Thoughts, Beliefs, and Walls?

Where are your thoughts? Where are your beliefs? Where are your walls? Are they in your head, your mind, your gut, or somewhere else? Throughout history, writers, scientists, religious leaders, philosophers, and psychologists have studied thinking but none have identified what makes up a thought and where does thinking begin or end. No one knows exactly what positive, negative, or neutral thoughts are or where and how they occur. In spite of this, the answers are important in psychology in order to help find ways to solve life problems.

In the early 1970s a new source for answers to these questions arrived in the West.

Traditional Chinese Medicine Arrives in the West

"Now, let me tell you about my appendectomy in Peking." So began the July 26, 1971, article by *New York Times* journalist James Reston, who accompanied Secretary of State Henry Kissinger on his historic trip to China. During this visit, Reston had emergency surgery in which acupuncture was used for pain control and thus a curious and astounded Western world had a glimpse into the mysteries of Eastern medicine as practiced in China.

Although a large Chinese population had immigrated and worked in the United States. during the 100 preceding years, relatively little was known at that time of traditional Chinese culture, medicine, or science outside their immigrant communities. Reston's personal experience and report, amplified by Kissinger's press briefings, changed this and his account, followed by President Richard Nixon's visit to China, captured the attention and curiosity of the American public.

The excitement rekindled the scientific interest in the human energy system that had lain dormant in Western medicine since the time of the Swiss physician Paracelsus who, in the sixteenth century, wrote about energy forces in medicine and the body's ability to heal itself. Energy medicine, which had been derailed time after time since the ancient Greek civilization, was to gain a significant toehold in the twenty-first century (Diepold, Britt and Bender, 2004).

The Physical You or the Energy You?

There was an old battle in Western medicine between two groups of scientists, the **vitalists** and the **mechanists.** The vitalists talked about life energy and energy systems as important to your well-being and the mechanists said that if you couldn't see the energy it couldn't be proved and therefore, it didn't exist. For reasons that were largely centered on personality and politics, the mechanists prevailed. They gathered evidence to support their theories of the brain from research on cadavers and as a result, many myths were perpetuated that lasted until this millennium. Among them was that the brain, once formed, could not continue to develop beyond the age of 16. Up until relatively recently, educators and psychologists were fairly pessimistic and believed the myth that the brain had too few connections and deteriorated before it even got past a person's teen years. However, recent studies have proven these beliefs untrue.

The Problem with Studying Cadavers

Imagine aliens coming to earth and finding a TV. They play with the TV remote and suddenly they get to see pictures and hear sounds from the TV itself. They are curious about where the pictures and sounds come from so they take the TV apart — no more images and sounds! They then put the TV together again and the pictures and sounds return. From this they might conclude that the pictures and sounds were inside the TV. However, we know that the TV receives and distributes signals through the airwaves or through cable connections that originate elsewhere. And, like aliens studying a television set, scientists who studied the brain in cadavers and theorized that the physical brain alone accounts for all the processes involved in thought, emotion, and behavior, also formed inaccurate conclusions as to how the mind functioned.

Myth: Your Brain Architecture Limits Your Thoughts and Actions

Philosophers and scientists had long debated whether the lack of control human beings have over their thoughts and emotions might be explained by what were defined as deficits in the brain's architecture and function (Koestler, 1967; Konner, 1982).

The science of the mid-twentieth century was pessimistic about what was described as a failure of the human brain for two reasons: the structure of the brain revealed by dissections and microscopic study pointed out a lack of connections or wiring between the physical parts of the brain popularly referred to as the **old, primitive brain** and the **new, evolved brain**. The **old brain** includes more primitive structures such as the midbrain and the limbic system. This area of your brain is responsible for basic life functions and the fight–flight-freeze stress response. The **new brain,** which includes the outer cerebral cortex of the brain, is more evolved and specializes in higher, more complex thought. The lack of connections between these two parts meant that there was little opportunity for the **new brain** (the part that allows you to do calculus and design complicated machinery) to help when the **old brain** was triggered in response to fear or stress.

William's story illustrates the idea of *primitive response* of his **old brain** disconnected from his **new brain**.

Example of Primitive Response

William is a 23-year-old medical student who is bright, funny, and a good guy who would give you the shirt off his back — except while he's driving. When someone in front of him is driving too slowly, especially an elderly person, he experiences "road rage." He responds by driving fast around the offending driver and giving him the finger. At one point an exchange in a parking lot over a parking space nearly cost him his life. He was quite shaken and says, "I know losing my temper in these situations is crazy, but I can't help it." What happens to William illustrates the problem with brain architecture; the ability to shift thoughts is dampened by out-of-control emotions and William's emotional reaction came from his **old brain** unregulated by his **new brain**, his thinking self.

There would be very few people left if everyone simply acted on a wish to kill someone when they were cut off, or felt disrespected by another driver. There needs to be a moment to think through the consequences of your actions, but it is often very difficult to take the time to connect to the higher thinking cortex when you're engaged in an emotional experience. It is further complicated by related beliefs you already have about the situation because of prior life experiences. William says, "I want to be able to say to myself that the old man driving so slowly on the road is just like my grandfather whom I love, but before I can think, the rage takes over me."

Generating New Pathways

This inability to gain control over runaway emotions poses a huge hurdle on an individual level. If there were no way to develop a path in the brain between thinking and feeling, then William is left without the ability to prevent his angry reaction to slow drivers and connect to the kind feelings he has toward his elderly grandfather. Beyond the individual level, there are also global implications. Lack of communication between the thinking part of being human and the emotional part of being human has resulted in wars and disruptions of civilization. These shortcomings of the brain's development have led some to predict the destruction of all humankind by our own hand. It is frightening to think that generations of traumatized, angry brains in war-torn countries are set for life, with no chance of healing and repair. Thankfully, since most of the information in Western science about the brain came initially only through dissection of cadavers, research such as the Nobel Prize winning studies of Eric Kandel (2007) and newer technology has allowed us a glimpse of the living brain which indicates you can indeed make new pathways and can also repair old ones.

Your Brain can Generate and Regenerate

New research and technology have reported that the living brain can continue to change with your thinking and these discoveries are quite relevant to overcoming self-defeating beliefs and behaviors. In recent years, scientists have discovered that your thoughts are able in a sense to "rewire" the physical brain so the brain's functioning is improved. In other words, you're not stuck with the original lack of wiring. Your brain has plasticity and it can change (Schwartz & Begley, 2002; Scott, 2006).

If your thoughts have the power to rewire your brain, the next compelling question is how? Researchers are investigating numerous possibilities and are now looking beyond **the physical you** for answers. This opens the door for investigation into what is considered **the energy you.**

The Energy You

As already discussed, until recently most of how we perceived **the energy you** has been in terms translated from Eastern medicine where **the energy you** was never separated from **the physical you.** Formulations of chakras, meridians, and biofields have provided the start of exploration into **the energy you** by Western mental health professionals, but they are only a beginning. Western medicine is being drawn back to its own history and researchers are now studying both **the physical you** and **the energy you** with studies and theories gleaned from not only biology but also physics. For example, psychologist Fred Gallo (2007) refers to Einstein's equation that depicts the relationship of energy and mass ($E=MC^2$) as a way for the Western world to conceptualize the statement that **energy you** and **physical you** are intertwined.

Western Interest in Energy and Wellness

In the West, centers to study complementary and alternative methods of health care have been developed at most medical schools due to a growing interest in and awareness of the benefits of Eastern practices for mental and physical healing, and overall well-being.

In addition to physicians, mental health professionals were also impressed by the clinical improvements accompanying Eastern practices that engaged the acupuncture meridian system and the chakras. This led to the formation of a branch of mental health known as *energy psychology*. Energy psychology is an umbrella term suggested by psychologist Fred Gallo in 1999 to include all psychologically oriented therapeutic strategies that incorporate the various forms of vibrational energetic influences and utilize the meridian system, the chakra system, or the area that surrounds the body called the biofields.

Energy psychology not only includes the important elements of establishing rapport with patients, setting goals and talking as practiced in traditional therapies, it also takes into account the energy of the patients' words, thoughts, and beliefs, and their impact on the mind-body-energy system. This attention to the flow of energy could be compared to the attention paid to the flow of air when there is a breathing problem. In CPR (cardiopulmonary resuscitation) the first step is to clear the airway, because no matter what else is done you cannot breathe until the blocked airway is cleared. Similarly, from an energy psychology perspective, you cannot resolve a psychological problem when your mind-body-energy system is blocked, until it is corrected.

Vibrational Frequencies and Fields

Even though energy was at one point part of Western medical history, it was difficult at first for Western scientists to think of the workings of the mind in energy terms. The physical brain seemed a more promising site for explanations of thoughts and beliefs over the unsubstantiated concepts of energy and invisible pathways.

However, in addition to the studies showing the brain regenerating and creating new pathways, there was the development of incredible technology that created an interface between the brain and computers. News of computers allowing individuals the use of artificial limbs directed by their own thoughts could not be ignored (Scott, 2006). If it was possible to create new pathways between parts of your brain and you could generate movement in a limb by your thoughts, the next natural step was to begin to study the nature of the energy required to do these mental-physical acts and explore where the energy came from.

Mind is More Than Brain

As early as the 1960s the famous brain surgeon, Wilder Penfield (1969) remarked that when all was known about the brain, we would still not know all there was to know about the mind.

Now, a growing body of research is supporting this idea. At the frontiers of research of the mind, scientists are suggesting that every cell in your body has some capacity to remember; and that failure to consider and treat "body memory" accounts for the continued power of a psychological trauma despite years of talk therapy (van der Kolk, 1994; Levine, 1997; Scaer, 2007)

Two examples of other parts of the body that have been given special consideration as sources for energetic processes related to mind are the heart and the fascia (a component of the connective tissue system in your body). When scientists talk about the roles of the heart and the fascia, they talk about electromagnetic fields and electronic signaling, both of which are forms of energy, and therefore are part of **the energy you.**

The Heart

It has been shown that the brain and heart are linked in a strong electromagnetic field generated by the heart (Pearsall, 1998). Studies have shown that the heart beats with inter-beat variability that is an indicator of your health and well-being (Childre, Martin & Beech, 1999). Other studies show that heart rate variability is influenced by emotions as well as a person's physical state (Serban-Schreiber, 2003).

The Fascia

The fascia is another area that has drawn a great deal of excitement in recent years. Fascia surrounds muscles, bones, organs, nerves, blood vessels, and other parts of the body. It is an uninterrupted sheet extending throughout the entire body that is known to maintain structural integrity and support and to provide protection from external forces. At one time fascia was viewed as merely something inconvenient that got in the way of surgeons when they were trying to get to other organs that needed their attention. But now, fascia is catching attention as a possible source of communication among organs by way of acting as an electrical signaling device through cellular communication (Church, 2007). We will talk more about this in Chapters Three and Nine.

Memory Bound in Thought Fields

Information bound in thought fields is another way of thinking about where your walls are located, and is the basis for TAB. Biologist Rupert Sheldrake (1995) wrote about biological information in fields and psychologist Roger Callahan conceived the idea of thoughts bound in fields (Callahan & Callahan, 1996).

Dr. Callahan, inspired by both physics and philosophy, described thought fields as invisible, nonphysical electromagnetic patterns in space binding energetically encoded information into a cohesive arrangement that affects human behavior, emotions, and experience. He developed a psychotherapy called thought field therapy, or the Callahan Techniques™, that treated unwanted information in thought fields. Building on Dr. Callahan's work and others, the BDB Group defined a thought field as...*an energetic bridge between thought, memory, and emotional experience that reaches beyond our conscious awareness* (Diepold, Britt & Bender, 2004, p. 116).

The simplest way to conceptualize thought fields is to think of them as similar to magnetic fields. Remember in school when you placed a magnet under a piece of paper and sprinkled iron filings or paperclips on top of the paper? The small filings or paperclips then arranged themselves in a pattern that outlined the magnet's field. In the same way, it is hypothesized that materials in your thought fields are able to arrange themselves and influence patterns of behavior.

Like those invisible magnetic fields, thought fields are invisible to the human eye and, unfortunately, unlike magnetic fields, the existence of thought fields is not demonstrable with present technology. Nevertheless, if you accept the hypothesis that when you think about your problem and have an emotional response and the response is by way of a connection to the thought field, you could then imagine that by activating the thought and the response at the same time, you might be able to develop a treatment to release the negative emotional charge connected to the thought.

Thinking about a problem in order to help resolve it is not a new idea; it is used in almost every school of psychology. What you do with what you are thinking is what is different in TAB. In TAB, while thinking about your problem, you will be learning a way to focus your intention and reduce or eliminate the signals in the associated thought field that are linked to self-defeating thoughts, beliefs, or behaviors. You will learn more about the signals in thought fields in the next chapter.

Concept of Mind in TAB

As discussed in the Introduction, TAB (Touch and Breathe) is an energy psychology that was developed as an adaptation of a professional treatment called evolving thought field therapy (Diepold, Britt & Bender, 2004) In TAB your mind includes your every cell and all the unexplained connections that make up who you are and that link you and your thoughts to the cosmos.

When you do TAB you will be using meridian treatment points connected to familiar areas of **the physical you,** such as the bladder, lungs, and heart. You will also be thinking about the problem you want to work on, in a way that connects you to the thought field that binds the thought or belief of that particular problem. This process can be thought of as similar to tuning into a particular station on your radio.

When you use TAB you will put your awareness on certain meridian treatment points and use the synergy of touch, breath, intuition, intention, and mindfulness to self-treat.

Why TAB Works When Positive Thinking Doesn't

You may have had the experience of having the best of intentions, trying positive thinking, repeating affirmations and not having any success eliminating the problem. It is important to understand that positive thinking is an energetic process that involves the higher centers of the brain, the mind and all of you in the context of the energetic universe. An uncompromised flow of energy is required in order for you to connect to your positive intentions and goals; if your energy is disrupted by a negative belief, or your thought field contains unwanted signals, you would not be able to connect the positive intention to achieve your goal. TAB frees up energy and allows you to keep your focus because you work energetically on the thoughts and beliefs that have divided your energy.

An interesting study by psychologists John Diepold and David Goldstein (2002) lends some support to this energetic theory. Drs.

Diepold and Goldstein did a brain mapping using the QEEG (quantitative electroencephalogram) to study the changes in a patient's brain before and after a single energy treatment session. Not only did the patient report feeling much better after the treatment, the QEEG showed substantial positive differences in the brain map.

Revisiting William's Story

The issue for William, the medical student with "road rage," was the sight of someone intruding in his space instantly connected to a primitive survival mechanism of fight. The thought that followed was, "I've got to teach this person a lesson." The thought itself is not the problem and it's not part of a belief about people in general. In fact, William's belief about people in general is that he wants to help them, which is why he is in medical school.

If William could buy some time he could eventually get to a thought such as, "Hey, he's only some old guy like my granddad." But William can't shift thought fields quickly enough before he acts on his rage. The thought, "I've got to teach this guy a lesson," is in a thought field that contains an emotional signal which William experiences as righteousness and rage and he cannot get to a more forgiving and understanding place while in the clutch of his emotions.

In order to reduce the signal in the thought field, "I've got to teach this guy a lesson," William has to take the signal connected to his emotion of rage out of the thought field. Using TAB, William focused on the thought of the old man cutting him off. He then followed the steps (that you will learn in later chapters) to take the energetic signal out of the thought that had bound him to his intense emotional reaction. Using TAB, he was able to work on the actual energy of the thought field.

What Happens to Thought When You do TAB?

Compare William's thought about being cut off to a wrinkled bed sheet. Think of the signal for rage as wrinkles in the sheet. Doing TAB could be compared metaphorically to ironing the wrinkles. When you press the wrinkles from a sheet, you still have a sheet, but without the wrinkles. When you remove the energetic signal for rage from the thought field, you still have a thought but without the debilitating emotion. You then find it easier to shift thought fields and consider your options for how to deal with a situation with rational choice, rather than knee-jerk reaction.

What Happens to Memory?

After using TAB, you can still remember what you want to remember; you keep memories you want or need, but you no longer have to be subjected to the unwanted emotion that accompanies the memories. For those distressful memories connected to trauma, you will still remember the incidents, but the emotional impact will be different and the memory will be far less distressing. Most patients report that after treatment they can remember the event without reliving it.

And What About Beliefs?

Beliefs are judgments made by your mind when interpreting life events. We call them blocking beliefs if they compromise your stated intentions to reach your goals. Blocking beliefs are typically negative, and usually start with the words "I" or "I am" (something bad). Examples include, "I am not smart enough to..." or "I will be laughed at if I attempt this."

It is sometimes possible for a blocking belief to seem positive when you first uncover it, such as "I deserve to have some fun" or "I am unsafe in a particular situation." In these examples the belief, "I deserve to have some fun," can appear to be a constructive belief, but it may be connected to the belief that I deserve to have fun no matter what the consequences (as frequently happens with addictive situations.) Or the belief that "I am unsafe and I need to protect myself" may be true in some cases, but it may become an overriding belief that leads you to limiting yourself. Once you decide to use TAB to treat these beliefs that no longer serve you, you will have the ability to make new choices and consider healthier beliefs.

Sally's Story Continued

Recall that Sally, who was unemployed, struggled with interviews. Whenever she was in an interview, her brain would get flooded with negative thoughts, resulting in her barely being able to respond to the interviewer with any more than yes or no answers. Sally had no idea why she reacted that way, but she became angry each time she did. However, when she asked herself, "When was the first time I felt like this?" she remembered being in seventh grade. She was running for president of her class and her opponent was a boy named Ronald, whose mother was a friend of her mother's. Ronald's mother had visited Sally's mom and asked Sally what she would do if she were elected president. Sally was open in her response and told details of her plan of action if she won. The following week, both presidential candidates were to give speeches. Ronald was first to speak; he stood up and proceeded to say almost word for word all the ideas Sally had shared with his mother. Sally was shocked, angry, ashamed, and hurt. She was so upset that she was unable to recover and say something when it was her turn. She sat down, humiliated. As Sally recalled that memory she realized that this past experience caused her current feelings of anger and fear when she was faced with the prospect of giving out information about herself and her ideas, which she knew and her audience didn't. She was scared of revealing things about herself. She was able to connect that experience with the manner in which she reacted during the job interview. She stated, "You just can't trust anyone." When asked what she believed about herself when she thought that you just can't trust anyone, she replied, "I am not safe if I reveal too much."

As you can see, Sally's problem started when she was a twelve-year-old girl trying to protect herself against experiencing the pain and embarrassment of having her ideas stolen. Over time, however, that belief stopped serving her and, in fact, compromised her ability to function, as evidenced by her poor performance in job interviews. Previously she had been unaware of the connection.

Therefore, the wall that you surround yourself with can start out as useful but if it grows unchecked it can snowball into self-sabotage, because of the negative beliefs generated by it. Walls and beliefs build on one another and a belief has the energy to block progress and thus create a wall. A wall can then prove you are inept, which, in turn, then creates a belief. Many negative beliefs that create walls during adulthood come from beliefs learned early on in life. Often, in childhood they were protective or soothing, but in adulthood they are often limiting and agonizing.

Sally now recognized that unresolved memories, beliefs and feelings from that seventh grade experience kept her trapped and didn't allow her to participate effectively in an interview. Remembering the source of a problem does not necessarily resolve it. Many people are all too painfully aware of where their negative beliefs come from, yet they are still trapped behind walls because of them. As already discussed, sometimes it is useful to try to understand where beliefs come from, but it is not essential to recall the source in order to get through the wall or clear the energy disruption. Although Sally had identified the beginning event, and now understood the source of her interview problem, that knowledge alone did not change the disturbing feelings connected to the memory of the betrayal, nor the belief that she was unsafe when questioned during an interview.

Sally had tried positive thinking, talking, and trying to change her behavior but none of these strategies were successful. With TAB, she was able to identify what about the interview situation connected energetically with her old memory of humiliation. She used the techniques of TAB, which you will learn in the coming chapters, in the following way: briefly, she did a polarity check (Chapter 7); she then asked herself for permission to work on the problem by self-test (Chapter 6) and began to identify and treat the meridian points that required attention. She created a healthier belief, "I am able to choose what I tell others safely." At the end of the treatment she strengthened the belief by doing a future performance exercise that you will learn in Chapter 11.

The TAB self-treatment took Sally 30 minutes. She went to her next interview and sat down without her usual anxiety. Although she did not get the position because she was told she was overqualified, she was delighted that she was able to show the interviewer how much she knew. She had reached her goal to perform well in an interview. A week later, another company called her for an interview having heard about her from the interviewer of the past week. Sally had moved forward, her thought field cleared of emotional signals that were no longer useful, and her wall was gone. This is quite typical of a TAB treatment, and once you decide to use TAB to treat beliefs that no longer serve you, you will have the ability to make new choices and consider healthier beliefs.

Exercise: Evaluate Your Walls

Here is an exercise that will help you begin to use this book. Take some time and respond to the following questions:

What walls or disruptions are you facing? What thoughts, beliefs and feelings are getting in your way? What behaviors do you want to change? How would you describe your "wall" or your "disruption"?

_____

_____

_____

What do you think you need to do to get past your problem?

_____

_____

_____

When did your problem start? What was going on in your life when the problem first appeared?

_____

_____

_____

When was your problem the worst? When did it cause the most difficulty for you?

_____

_____

_____

What memories do you associate with this problem?

_____

_____

_____

_____

_____

Was it ever useful to have this problem? If yes, when?

_____

_____

_____

Is there an "I" or "I am" belief that goes with this problem? If yes, when did it start?

_____

_____

_____

Moving on to Chapter Two

Summarizing this chapter, you now can think about your problem thoughts and behaviors in terms of the energy of walls and beliefs. Next you will learn more about the nature of beliefs and the triggers that set off your unwanted thoughts and behaviors as signals in the thought fields.

CHAPTER 2

Understanding What is in Your Thought Fields

In order to understand what you will be doing when you treat your problem with TAB, it is useful to look at the nature of beliefs and what is in your thought fields.

In this chapter you will focus on the energy of thoughts in thought fields and the fundamentals of blocked energy in negative beliefs. The energy of beliefs will be likened to filters through which your thoughts and experiences pass. You will understand how pieces of an old memory can energetically cheat you out of having an objective reaction to your life in the present, even if a new situation only resembles the old one in a minor way. You will also learn how even a small overlap between old and new experiences can compromise your life and bring about unwanted thoughts, feelings, and behaviors in two ways: blocking beliefs and triggers.

We will also define and discuss three types of "signals" (the energy of thoughts connected to unwanted emotions) called *perturbations*, *elaters*, and *harmonizers*. When these signals continue past their usefulness, you will want to quiet them, metaphorically iron them out, using TAB, which will allow you the opportunity to shift your thoughts and widen your choices about how to react when struggling with self-defeating beliefs and behaviors.

To help you track your progress, you will learn two measurement systems, Subjective Unit of Disturbance/Distress (SUD) and Subjective Unit of Elation/Enjoyment (SUE). These measurement systems will allow you to assess the strength of an emotional signal in your particular thought field and in this way you will be able to judge where you are in your self-work.

At the end of the chapter you will review more questions that ask you to define your problem(s) in terms of the triggers, emotions, and beliefs experienced.

Understanding the Role of Beliefs

Beliefs are thoughts that influence what you think about yourself and the world you live in and they can either be reasonable and logical, or unreasonable and illogical and they may be positive or negative. You may be painfully aware of a belief and its influence on your life, or you may be totally unaware and may be surprised to discover the beliefs that lie just below your consciousness. In TAB you are working on beliefs that compromise your energy system, shut you down, and block you from considering your choices. Once your energy system is blocked, you have limited ability to consider your choices when you react to a situation. *Blocking beliefs* act as filters for how you take in all the information about the world and disrupt your ability to use your intention and positive thinking because of their influence on your energy flow.

Core Beliefs

Beliefs that hold deep meaning and are usually solidly in place are called *core beliefs*. Core beliefs relate to the self and usually, but not always, begin with the statement, "I" or "I am..." The earlier they begin in life, the stronger they are in adulthood. For example, if your parents are angry at each other and take it out on you by saying you are a bad child, you may develop a core belief that "I am bad" and the rest of your life may be experienced through that lens. Again, you may be aware of how a core belief limits your life or you could be totally surprised because the effects of a negative core belief are at times quite subtle.

Many of the beliefs you have when you are young are incorrect, but not all of these are core beliefs; noncore beliefs are easily changed as you progress through life. These beliefs often start early in life, but with new information or education your beliefs change. For example, Jill, a 22-year-old college graduate was offered a job in a small computer company, but the starting salary was low. While she really wanted to take the job, she knew she could not afford to live on that salary. When it was suggested that she ask her potential employer for a higher starting salary, she was surprised. Her belief was that salaries were not negotiable, plus it was impolite to talk about money. Given new information, and really desiring the new position, she was able to speak up and ask for a higher amount. She was pleased when the employer agreed with her request.

Compare Jill's belief to Alexandra's.

Alexandra's Story

Alexandra is a 46-year-old professor of Slavic languages at a prestigious university. Alexandra has remained unmarried, though not by choice. She described it as, "I keep finding nasty men. I am like a bad-guy magnet. The only ones I attract are those who ignore my needs and use me until they find the right one. I spend many lonely nights." Alexandra was acutely aware that she was getting older and the situation was getting worse, but she seemed to have no way to stop herself from a sense of neediness even when she knew the person she was with was an emotional disaster for her.

When thinking about growing up, she remembered being six years old when her parents, both college professors, finally split up. They originally met in Russia, where her American mother had gone to study briefly and met her Russian father. Her mother fell head over heels in love and, through the marriage, had provided the means for her husband to come to the United States. Alexandra described her parent's fights, which were always in Russian, as intense and frightening. She recalled her father's venom as he called her mother too smart for her own damn good and then her father would glare at Alexandra and say, "You, you're no better." After the divorce, her dad remarried a Russian woman with a daughter Alexandra's age. Alexandra related some of her father's last words to her before he left her life completely. "My dad would rarely visit me and when he did he'd bring a picture of his new daughter and tell me things like, 'See how pretty she is. She doesn't need to be smart. No man wants a smart woman. That's the problem with you and your mother.'"

Alexandra loved school and went on to a solid career but she carried with her the blocking belief that she was defective because she was too smart, and therefore, unlovable. Once she had made the decision to be smart she then believed that she could not be attractive to a smart man. She looked at life through the lens of "I am not good enough," and it permeated every friendship and every relationship.

These stories demonstrate the differences between noncore beliefs and core beliefs. In Jill's case, her belief was easily shifted upon gaining the knowledge that it was completely acceptable to ask for a higher starting salary, whereas Alexandra's belief was part of her core identity.

You will learn more about blocking beliefs in Chapters 8 and 9, where you will learn ways to check for and self-treat them. The questions that end this chapter are designed to help you begin to become aware of these blocking beliefs and how they may influence your choices in the present.

Triggers

Triggers in energy psychology can be considered forces that instantly link a present day event to a memory and the associated feelings, whether or not you are aware of a connection. The theory is that triggers create or result in energy signals that are the source of your emotions and drive both wanted and unwanted behaviors, as you will find in the examples later in the chapter.

Sometimes you think that a wall or unwanted emotion is gone, but then a new situation reminds you that it still affects you. How does that happen? The answer is in part because of triggers. You probably have experienced how vividly a thought or smell brings back a particular memory and associated feelings. For instance, in hypnosis, the smell of a baby blanket is sometimes used to help trigger childhood experiences. Anniversaries of occasions both good and bad are well-known triggers. An anniversary of a positive life event, such as a celebration, can trigger feelings of joy and happiness. An anniversary of a negative life event, such as a bad accident, can trigger feelings of sadness or loss.

Seemingly Innocuous Events Can Be Triggers

Triggers can be seemingly innocuous. The returning veteran who cannot take his children to the local fireworks, or the young mother who can no longer drive her car without terror after she had a car accident, are common examples. Even a simple reminder mailed to you for a yearly medical or dental checkup can connect to memories of a past illness, a loved one's death, or a painful dental procedure.

Nasir's Story

Nasir, a volunteer for a research study at a university medical school, was shocked at the level of disturbance that he felt when he entered the room with the magnetic resonance imaging (MRI) scanner used in the study. It was so intense that he couldn't lie on the table and enter the enclosure to be scanned. He then became aggravated with himself and while sitting up on the table repeatedly told the technician how ridiculous he felt. He said, "I just have to do it. I feel stupid to be wasting everyone's time like this." The rest of the research team outside the scan room could hear his comments and decided to ask whether the situation reminded him of anything. At first, he said, "No," but when asked to really search his memory for another similar situation, he thought again. Then with a shaking voice he explained that he had been with his wife through many MRI scans as she battled cancer.

Nasir's wife had lost the battle and he had unconsciously connected the scanning machine and her dying. The MRI scanner was a negative trigger of memories, thoughts, and emotions associated with the loss of his wife. Nasir had experienced the sudden emotional power and force of a seemingly benign experience as it triggered a very meaningful and painful memory.

Triggers Can Be Mysterious

Professional writers understand triggers and the part they play in self-defeating thoughts and behaviors. They describe triggers in detail in order to develop their characters and story lines. They use them to explain otherwise unexplainable behaviors by their characters. They know that the use of the right trigger can draw you into the plot because they hold a reader fascinated. Movie producer Alfred Hitchcock was famous for his use of triggers to explain mysterious behaviors from his heroes. For example, in *Spellbound* the hero panics when he sees ski tracks in the snow and the moviegoer is left to guess what triggers this incomprehensible terror. Later, as the hero regains the lost memory, we find out that as a boy he was part of an accident and witnessed the death of his younger brother. The accident involved a fence and was stored in his unconscious as a pattern of lines; every time he saw this pattern it triggered feelings of horror though he couldn't remember the actual source.

Triggers Can Be Intentional Cues

Triggers are frequently thought out and planned to provide reminders of happy times. One of the most popular triggers is the music a bride and groom select for their first dance together. The song is planned so that in the future whenever it is played it reminds the couple of all the sights, sounds, and good feelings of their wedding day.

Avoiding negative triggers and developing positive ones as reminders often become critically important when you are dealing with unwanted habits that are pleasurable. When triggers are conscious rather than unconscious, which means when you are aware of triggers, you are less surprised by them and can take precautions. For example, some cigarette smokers say that an urge to have a cigarette is so connected with having a cup of coffee that this urge often arises with the mere smell of coffee. In order to quit successfully, professionals often advise you to avoid coffee and other places where you've enjoyed smoking most in order to avoid succumbing to the negative trigger. They also suggest that putting a picture of your family in the place where you normally carry your cigarettes serves as a positive trigger so you can reach for it when you want to reach for a cigarette. Triggers like these act as intentional cues to help with problem resolution.

The Three Major Components of Thought Fields

The experience of emotional signals in the thought fields connects you with your blocking beliefs and triggers. During these times when you are feeling strong emotions, you can capitalize on this opportunity and focus your intention on shifting your problem by using the techniques of TAB.

Your thought field can be about real or imagined experiences that have a direct effect on your physical, emotional, and energetic state of being. This means that your thought fields have pieces of information that you understand on an emotional or a "feeling level." Emotions are the feelings connected with thoughts. There is also an important relationship in reverse: you will also have thoughts connected to feelings. Thoughts connect to your feelings as you are reminded of prior experiences with similar feelings.

You may be asking yourself if triggers can be everywhere and associated with just about anything, depending on your life experiences how can you ever do anything about them? And why would you ever want to change triggers for positive feelings? In order to answer these questions it is first necessary to think about different types of triggers in the thought field.

There are three kinds of emotional signals:

1. *Perturbations* are connected to negative emotions (rage, grief, shame, etc.)

2. *Elaters* are connected to positive emotions (happiness, joy, etc.)

3. *Harmonizers* are connected to emotions that empower your innate healing wisdom and a universal healing wisdom and peace.

Perturbations

Perturbations are the signals in a thought field that are related to very unpleasant and disturbing feelings or trauma. Psychologist Roger Callahan (Callahan & Callahan, 1996) first introduced the concept of perturbations as the source of the experience of negative emotions.

Of all your varied emotional signals, perturbations rule; they trump the rest. Negative emotions are not necessarily bad; in fact, some of them help you survive. It is essential to have the emotions of fear and anger warn you of danger and the need to defend yourself when you are threatened in a particular moment. For example, if you were going to your car in a dark, deserted parking lot, you would want to pay attention to your gut feeling to hurry to your car and get quickly in and lock the doors. However, if these emotions keep going after the danger has passed, you are safely in your car and your heart is still racing and you can't quiet down, they can be destructive to your mind and body. You can think of them as an alarm clock; once you are aware of the time, you should turn off the alarm; otherwise it rings all day and becomes a distraction that gets in the way. Frequently, strong emotions get triggered in situations where there is no current survival issue. For example, William's road rage described in the last chapter does not serve any survival purpose, yet it is an extremely intense emotion that has previously gotten him into serious trouble in a related altercation.

Negative life events and their connected negative emotions are part of the human experience, as illness is part of the human experience. Similarly, you have a natural system that allows you to heal emotional upsets, and in the same way you have an immune system that allows healing of physical ailments in your life. Normally, a bad thing happens, you respond to it, and then the bad thing fades into the past and becomes a story. You put the experience in perspective. The memory can still be important, but thinking about it is no longer a cause of intense distress. This is analogous to how the immune system keeps your health in check by fighting off millions of bacteria that enter your body on a daily basis. It is only when situations compromise or overload the emotional immune system that things get out of control.

Elaters

Elaters are the signals in a thought field related to enjoyment, pleasure and the release of built-up tension. Psychologist John Diepold developed the concept of elaters and defined them as the energy signals within the thought field that influence the experience of positive emotions and sensations such as joy, happiness, and enjoyment (Diepold, Britt & Bender, 2004). Elaters reward you with good feelings. They are the fun parts of life that drive and maintain the excitement of living. But just as the persistence of perturbations in a thought field beyond their usefulness can be self-destructive, elaters can also lead to destructive behaviors when they are unchecked or when they become part of an escape from disturbing or difficult life circumstances. As discussed in the last chapter, elaters are problematic when used to escape the present moment and/or make you unable to deal with important life functions.

Pleasant emotions have been studied less than unpleasant ones and there are many unanswered questions about the human experience of pleasant emotions (Averill & More, 2004; Diepold, Britt & Bender, 2004). However, researchers are now asking: Are there fewer pleasant emotions than unpleasant ones? Does the weakening of pleasant emotions over time cause the experience of boredom? Are elaters that continue and become addictive the results of painful perturbations in another thought field? Although all of these questions cannot be answered within the scope of this book, you will learn how to deal with unwanted elaters (such as addictions) using TAB.

Harmonizers

Harmonizers are the signals in a thought field that connect you to the experience of calm and tranquility. John Diepold defined harmonizers as the experience of emotions that cause you to feel a sense of "in the moment," "mindful," and a feeling of being in balance (Diepold, Britt & Bender, 2004.) He compared it to a state that some people refer to as enlightenment in which you have an expansive, intuitive grasp of meaning and mind. Harmonizers signal and influence feelings of peacefulness and unconditional love and they are the energetic signals that connect to and carry universal and innate healing wisdom. The concept of harmonizers in the thought field implies poise, self-control and equilibrium that are reflected in your energetic, emotional, and physical states. When your thought fields are free of active perturbations and elaters, harmonizers in the thought field produce the experience of well-being. There is harmony and congruence in your feeling, action, thought, and health and it is in this state that your natural abilities for intuition and healing thrive.

The influence of harmonizers on thoughts can be both subtle and profound. Certain times or events that evoke harmonizers can literally take your breath away and lead to descriptors such as "breathless" or "awesome." It might be the first time you successfully rode a bike, your first view of the Grand Canyon, or the first time holding your newborn child. Harmonizers also exist in day-to-day connections, but are largely ignored because they are drowned out by the distress of perturbations or the excitement of elaters. There is potential for harmonizers in every bicycle ride and every time you sit at the dinner table with a loved one. It will become easier to connect to harmonizers in your thought fields as you clear away unwanted elaters and perturbations.

The Candy Cane Effect

In considering how perturbations and elaters relate to one another and contribute to energy disruptions, the analogy of a candy cane is useful. The colors of a candy cane are woven together in a way that is difficult to separate the places where one color stops and the other begins. *The Candy Cane Effect* (Dr. Diepold personal communication September 2006) is a way of describing the intertwining of your good feelings associated with elaters, your bad feelings associated with perturbations, and the difficulties you face when dealing with self-sabotaging, self-defeating thoughts and behaviors that result from their entanglement. Let's re-examine Teresa's Story.

The Candy Cane Effect in Teresa's Story

You met Teresa in Chapter 1: she's a marketing executive and single mom with young children, and she is involved in out-of-control, addictive computer game playing. The perturbations in her thought fields were the signals that made her feel overwhelmed, unloved, uncared for, and depressed. The elaters were the connections to the fun and distraction of *"mindless me"* time. The elaters were not a problem in and of themselves as it's fun to play games on the computer. The problem was Teresa couldn't stop and her sleep and general well-being were suffering. The time spent on the computer took away from her time with her children and her job and caused her to have even more perturbations in her thought field connected to being a bad mother and a bad employee.

Treating the Perturbations and Elaters

Teresa needed to treat both the disturbing and the enjoyable signals in the thought field; she needed to use TAB to treat both the perturbations and elaters. You may be asking yourself why should Teresa treat the elaters, why shouldn't she be able to enjoy herself? The answer is that Teresa will still be able to enjoy herself, but enjoyment had to be signaled by a healthier activity than the one at the computer. Once

Teresa treated the elating signal connected to using the computer for mindless escape, she was able to shift thought fields; without the addictiveness of the elating signal, she had the option to choose to gain enjoyment by sleep and a healthy night's rest.

In other words, Teresa could still have the thought of wanting to play a game on her computer, but she used the TAB process to energetically smooth out the elaters in the thought field that kept her a prisoner to playing the game without an option to stop. Whenever elaters are quieted in a thought field, the potential for harmonizer signals to be experienced is increased.

Paying Attention to Positive Emotions

Paying attention to your pleasant, positive emotions, as well as the unpleasant, negative ones, is extremely important for gaining control over any addictive, excessive, or out-of-control repetitive behaviors like smoking, nail-biting, continual hand washing and endless computer game playing. Rather than simply thinking of these problems as *disorders* or perturbations, it is important to consider them as *"in orders"* or elaters (Diepold, Britt & Bender, 2004). In other words, you are thinking this way or behaving that way *in order to* feel good or *in order to* avoid feeling bad. Traditional forms of psychotherapy emphasize unpleasant thoughts and emotions when treating unwanted or self-defeating behaviors, often without considering the pleasure that the self-destructive behavior might bring in the short-term; this is treating only one of the colored stripes of the candy cane. They tend to ignore the pleasant emotions, the second color stripe of the candy cane, that sustain the hook keeping you trapped in a self-sabotaging pattern because it feels good.

In Chapter One, you answered some basic questions to get started. Look back at these now and review your answers. As you think about the disruptions or blocks in your energy consider the signal possibilities that could account for the difficulties — both elaters and perturbations. You will also want to consider whether there is a candy cane effect or combination of the signals.

Measuring Your Progress

On a long road trip you often follow signs that indicate how many more miles until you reach your destination. It is reassuring to have indications of where you are and how much farther you have to go. Similarly, you will use three scales to measure your progress in TAB. We will discuss the first two (SUD and SUE scales) in this chapter and the third (SUFI scale) in Chapter 11. The SUD scale (Subjective Units of Disturbance) and the SUE scale (Subjective Units of Elation) are very useful because they help you track how you're feeling from start to finish.

Zero to Ten Scales

Again, like following the posted miles on a road trip, when you begin anything new, in this case inner healing work, it is helpful to know where you are so that you can track your progress. Research professionals in all areas of science use scales to document their procedures and evaluate the outcomes of experimental studies. Medical professionals have used similar zero to ten response scales when asking patients to rate pain or discomfort level before or during treatment procedures.

The SUD and SUE are both zero to ten scales for tracking your progress in self-treatment. It is not unusual for you sometimes to forget how bad things were in the beginning of treatment because you are feeling better; therefore, it is reinforcing for you to get an idea about how far you've come in your self-treatment by following your progress on a zero to ten scale. You should find that SUD and SUE measures go down quickly when working with energy techniques such as TAB. If they do not, it is an indication of a problem or a belief that is blocking your progress. You will learn how to deal with this situation, when it arises, in Chapters 7 and 8.

The SUD Scale:
Subjective Units of Disturbance, Distress or Upset

The SUD scale measures your level of disturbance when thinking about a problem and is a way to connect with perturbations in the thought field. The SUD level is a convenient scaling method devised by psychiatrist Joseph Wolpe (1966) that was simplified over time to a zero to ten scale. It is called a *subjective* scale because it is based on your own perception of your feeling and is one of the most widely used scales in psychotherapy. You will use the SUD scale when you want to rate how upset or disturbed you are feeling when you think about the problem you want to treat. When using the SUD scale, ask yourself, "When I think of my problem how upset (disturbed or distressed) am I *right now* on a scale of zero to ten, with zero being no disturbance or upset and ten being the highest or worst disturbance possible?" (See the SUD Scale below — Box 2.1) It is important to notice that you are being asked to rate how disturbed you are feeling when you think about the problem in the *present moment,* not in the past.

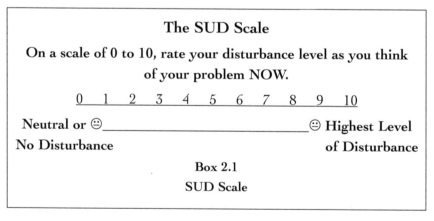

The SUD Scale

On a scale of 0 to 10, rate your disturbance level as you think of your problem NOW.

0   1   2   3   4   5   6   7   8   9   10

Neutral or ☺_____☺ Highest Level
No Disturbance   of Disturbance

Box 2.1
SUD Scale

Self-treatment Goal in SUD level

Your level of disturbance is caused by perturbations in your thought field. It is possible to clear the thought field of perturbations completely and reach a SUD level of zero. In order to maintain balance, once you clear perturbations and lower your SUD level, you should also clear elaters associated with certain behaviors. For that you will need the SUE score.

The SUE Scale:
Subjective Units of Elation or Enjoyment Scale

John Diepold developed the SUE scale to parallel the SUD scale, but instead of measuring disturbance, it measures your sense of enjoyment or pleasure derived from a particular thought or behavior that you know on some level is not good for you. The SUE scale (subjective units of elation or enjoyment) was designed for use when you are working on self-defeating behaviors signaled by elaters in the thought field (i.e., the joy or rush of smoking, or the mental rest of computer game playing.) The SUE scale assesses the strength of these elating signals connected to unwanted behaviors such as nail-biting, uncontrolled computer game playing, and smoking. (See Box 2.2 below)

The SUE Scale

Rate your enjoyment level with the SUE scale.

0   1   2   3   4   5   6   7   8   9   10

Neutral or ☺_____☺ **Highest Level**

No Enjoyment   **of Enjoyment**

Box 2.2
The SUE Scale

When using this scale you can ask yourself one or both of the following questions:

1. On a scale of zero to ten with zero being no enjoyment or neutral and 10 being the highest degree of enjoyment or pleasure I can imagine, when I imagine continuing the behavior I want to eliminate even though it is not good for me, how great is my enjoyment?

2. On a scale of zero to ten with zero being no enjoyment or neutral and 10 being the highest degree of enjoyment or pleasure I can imagine, when I imagine continuing the behavior I want to eliminate

and even though I know what it costs me and others, how great is my enjoyment?

Exercise: The Candy Cane of Your Story

Worksheet Instruction

Worksheet 2.1

Consider the problem(s) you thought about in Chapter 1 (or different ones if you prefer) in terms of triggers, perturbations, elaters, and blocking beliefs. Don't worry if you draw a blank on some questions, either guess or leave them unanswered. Use the following guide to sort out the issues.

At the end of the last chapter you wrote a negative belief about yourself. Write it again. (Usually a belief starts out with "I am..."or "I...")

_____

_____

_____

What are situations or things that act as triggers for this problem?

_____

_____

_____

Describe any negative or positive emotions or thoughts associated with this problem.

_____

_____

_____

Do you have self-sabotaging behaviors because of your problem? If yes, describe the behaviors.

_____

_____

_____

Do any of the self-sabotaging behaviors feel good or help you escape the present moment?

_____

_____

_____

(Hint: If there is a "feel good" quality to the self-sabotage, you have elaters in the thought field.)

Do any of the self-sabotaging behaviors relieve you of tension? Does the tension immediately rebuild when you stop the behavior?

_____

_____

(Hint: Tension relief usually means perturbations and elaters are in the thought field.)

Do any of the self-sabotaging behaviors involve significant others?

_____

_____

Using the SUD scale:

"When I think of this problem how upset (disturbed or distressed) am I *right now* on a scale of zero to ten with zero being no disturbance or upset and ten being the highest or worst disturbance possible?"

_____

Using the SUE scale:

On a scale of zero to ten with zero being no enjoyment or neutral and ten being the highest degree of enjoyment or pleasure I can imagine, when I imagine continuing the behavior I want to eliminate, and knowing it is not good for me, how great is my enjoyment? _____

On a scale of zero to ten with zero being no enjoyment or neutral and ten being the highest degree of enjoyment or pleasure I can imagine, when I imagine continuing the behavior I want to eliminate, and knowing what it costs me and others, how great is my enjoyment?

_____

If your wall was broken down or your problem no longer existed, what changes would you like to see in your behavior in the future?

_____

_____

_____

Moving on to Chapter Three

In summary, you now have a way to think about your beliefs, emotions and thoughts energetically. Unwanted beliefs are composed of energy that could actually create disruptions in your energy system. Emotions and behaviors are a result of energetic signals in thought fields. In the next chapter you will learn more about TAB, and begin to learn how to the use the tools of touch, breath, mindfulness, intention and intuition in order to balance your energetic system and free yourself from limiting thoughts and beliefs.

CHAPTER 3

Components of TAB

I n this chapter, we will discuss the components of TAB and explain how in combination they will empower you to focus your intentions in a way that can create change. We will teach you how the meridian system, mindfulness, touch, breath, intention, and intuition each relate to TAB. In addition, you will learn an exercise for relaxation and focus in order to be in the moment to prepare you for being mindful while doing TAB.

Buddhism and Mindfulness

At the same time that Traditional Chinese Medicine was making inroads into Western medicine, Buddhist traditions, such as *mindfulness* and awareness of mind and body and being in the moment were also entering the scene and making a mark on Western concepts of health. Information about the usefulness of *mindfulness* for promoting well-being has come through the writings and teachings of the Dalai Lama, the exiled spiritual leader of Tibet; Thich Nhat Hahn, a Vietnamese Zen Buddhist monk; and was furthered by the research of Jon Kabat-Zinn, PhD of the University of Massachusetts Medical School.

The Development of Integrative Medicine

In the last decades, Traditional Chinese Medicine and the Buddhist methods which include acupuncture, acupressure, herbal medicine, tai chi, meditation and mindfulness have emerged on the scene as a component of health care and well-being choices. Most major U.S. medical schools and teaching hospitals have established alternative, complementary, and integrative medicine departments to explore and regulate the clinical practices and develop research for a growing accumulation of information on healing traditions from diverse sources and cultures.

Three important threads are evident:

- mind and body are inseparable;

- life energy circulates in you in some way similar to the system that circulates blood;

- the life energy system is influenced and strengthened, just as your cardiac system is influenced and strengthened by certain activities.

The activities that enhance your life energy include body positioning and breathing techniques such as tai chi, Qigong (sometimes known as chi gong), yoga and hula. Others involve changing your body's energy from the inside, for example using herbs or homeopathic medications, or from the outside by passing hands over energy sites as in Healing Touch and Reiki, using magnets or sounds, craniosacral therapy, or placing acupuncture needles (Gerber, 1988).

Gateway of TAB

TAB integrates components of Traditional Chinese Medicine, Buddhist mindfulness, and Western advances with touch, intention, and intuition. Like other energy psychologies, TAB requires a gateway to your energy system. While energy psychology methods use different systems, such as the chakras or biofields to treat psychological problems, in TAB you will use treatment points from twelve meridians and two vessels from the acupuncture meridian system. As we discussed in Chapter 1, meridians are channels that circulate the life energy, or chi, throughout the body. When the chi is flowing freely through these meridians the body is healthy and balanced, but if the life energy becomes blocked or stagnated, it can result in physical, mental, or emotional dis-ease. These meridians are named for parts of your physical body such as the bladder, gall bladder, stomach, thyroid, small intestines, lung, pericardium, heart, liver, spleen, large intestines and kidney. The two vessels from acupuncture system that we will use in TAB are called the governing vessel and the central vessel.

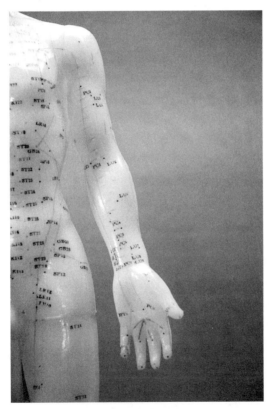

Picture 3.1
Acupuncture Meridians

In TAB you touch treatment points while taking at least one full mindful breath. You may choose to take as many breaths as you want on each selected treatment point. You will use your intention and intuition as you learn what parts of your energy system need your attention.

Touch

The first part of Touch and Breathe (TAB) is touch. Touch is as important to your physical and emotional well-being as breath, water, and food. The skin is the largest organ of the body. Research shows that infants who are not held by their caregivers fail to thrive and many die without human touch and contact (Field, 2001; see also Ornish, 1999). Recently, organizations such as the Touch Research Institute at the University Of Miami School of Medicine have been formed to study the effects of touch. In addition to the simple kinesthetic property of touch to the outer skin, studies are now being developed to investigate the effects of touch on the fascia, the layer beneath the skin that forms a matrix of tissue that connects all parts of the body. Although the importance of fascia has been well known and appreciated by occupational therapists, physical therapists, massage professionals, and those involved in craniosacral work, the investigative interest of researchers has opened the possibility to better understand its involvement in illness and healing (First International Fascia Congress, Boston, 2007).

Touch is Powerful

You are already familiar with the energy of touch. It's electric! Ask anyone who has ever been "in love." Take a moment and think of a time when you were "in love" and your significant other touched you, and you instantly felt warmth beyond words. Contrast that to the feel of the same person's touch if you had "fallen out of love." You can feel the difference, though it may be indescribable.

Touch is also evident in nonemotional experiences, though this activity is not generally apparent. You have all experienced static electric shocks after walking across a carpeted floor on a winter's night and then touching a doorknob or greeting a friend. This startling but harmless shock is an energy exchange.

However, touch is more than simple energy transfer; its effects can be enhanced in a variety of ways, including focusing your attention on your breath and thoughts. Touch is not only experienced in the mind of the person being touched, it is also experienced in the mind of the person doing the touching.

Touch Affects Meridian Points

TAB requires that you lightly touch and maintain contact with the acupuncture meridian point while taking at least one full breath in and out. Physicist William A. Tiller (1997) describes acupuncture points (meridian points) as a set of antenna elements with capabilities that exceed the most advanced radar system available today. In other words, touching a meridian activates your ability to tune into the energy of your thought fields. TAB allows controlled connection to the energy of both negative and positive thoughts, emotions and experiences. Each time you mindfully tune into your thoughts and feelings, you are learning more and more how to connect to your own inner healing processes. TAB enables your entire body to extend the antenna capabilities of your meridian system.

Breath

Breath is powerful. Breath is life. Yoga and tai chi combine breath and body postures in order to enhance health and well-being. In the Judeo-Christian tradition, life is said to come about as a result of God's breath and intention. In the Old Testament's book of *Genesis* (2:7) you read, "And the Lord God formed man of the dust of the ground, and breathed into his nostrils the breath of life; and man became a living being." Breath, inspiration, and expiration, creates and maintains life.

When you use the breath in TAB we suggest that you take a slow, deep inhalation through your nose, bringing air first into the abdomen, then filling the lungs and the chest cavity. When you exhale through your nose, you should empty the lungs first, then the abdomen. Use your nose rather than your mouth to breathe if it is comfortable, and pay attention to the vibrations caused by both the sound of your breath and the beat of your heart. We will discuss this further in the section below on mindfulness.

Intention

Much is being written in popular literature today about the role and power of intention to achieve your goals, but it is not clear what intention is. In TAB, intention is the energy you have that enables you to reach a goal. A good analogy could be a flashlight because when you direct the flashlight in the direction you want to go, it acts as a guide for you to follow. If the flashlight is covered or held at a poor angle you cannot see the path clearly.

Focused energy is powerful and according to Dr. Tiller (1997), if you could make the light from a 60-watt light bulb completely coherent (all focused on the same point) you would have a laser that was strong enough to bore through the sun. Now imagine that the power of your intention, if tightly focused, could bore its way through any negative thought, belief, and unwanted behavior.

Dr. Tiller (1997) further maintains that breath is the carrier of intention, which is why combining a deep breath with your intention is such an important component of TAB.

Intention and Affirmation

As described, when you make a statement of your intention you have an end purpose, a direction and a goal for healing, such as "I intend to conquer my problem of..." Your primary concerns are toward your future, but sometimes the energy of your intention is blocked. There are a variety of reasons why statements of intention can be blocked energetically, and in TAB there are ways to release the blocks. One method to help unblock your energy and clear the path for a statement of intention is using affirmations. Affirmations are statements that you use to recognize that you have a problem and accept your current position. For example, if your problem is with relationships, your affirmation could be "I accept myself even though I believe I don't deserve a healthy relationship." Compare affirmations and intentions to the little map at the mall that says, "You are here." Affirmations are you are here; statements of intention are where you want to be. It is especially important when you say an affirmation that you say it with a sense of acceptance of yourself, because the vibrational energy of acceptance is healing. If you are unable to say it with acceptance, you will learn how to treat that problem in Chapters 8 and 9.

Intuition

TAB is not only a means to help you focus your intention, it also a way to increase your intuitive ability.

The Art of Knowing

Intuition is your sense of knowing, and goes beyond the five senses that we usually use, and is often referred to as your sixth sense. In a spiritual context it has been referred to as connecting to the still voice within you or to the presence of a higher power. Everyone has some intuitive ability, and as with most skills, you can develop it further. People who interact with their energy system with practices such as Qigong, tai chi, yoga, energy psychology, and Reiki frequently find that their intuition becomes stronger and stronger.

It is the intuitive process that ultimately guides your TAB treatment and helps you notice which meridian sites require special attention for treatment. Some people experience this as simply a "knowing"; or describe it as "a meridian point just 'popped' into my head." Others report visualizing either the treatment site or focus area when thinking about their problem. The *focus areas* are the physical parts of your body that correlate with the treatment points you will be using. (We will further discuss focus areas in Chapter 10.)

Mindfulness in TAB

Mindfulness is a technique in which a person brings one's awareness back from the past or from the future, in order to become aware of his or her thoughts and actions in the present moment, for it is only in the present moment that you can analyze thoughts nonjudgmentally. Mindfulness is well recognized in Eastern and Western traditions, and has attracted a great deal of interest recently among Western mental health professionals as a nonpharmacological means of dealing with anxiety and depression.

Mindfulness is a practice that can be done at any time, and in TAB you will learn a mindful way to treat walls, thoughts, triggers, negative beliefs, and energy disruptions. Techniques to enhance mindfulness could fill volumes, so we will just teach you some that are important to TAB. Your awareness will be drawn to your breath and the exchange of energy that passes through the 'center of self' and the palm side of your hands. The 'center of self' includes every cell of your body, the meridian treatment points and their corresponding focus areas, and your connection to the universe and beyond. As you use these treatments, we ask that you focus with an attitude of acceptance for where you are today and an appreciation for your willingness to make changes.

Exercise for Mindfulness

The following exercise is practice for the direction of your attention and increasing mindfulness when doing TAB.

Exercise for Being in the Moment

While comfortably seated, with both of your feet on the floor, place your hands, with palms up, on your lap. (See Picture 3.2)

Picture 3.2

Mindfulness

Set your awareness on the palms of your hands and have in your mind (brain, heart, every cell of body and infinite universe) an intention that you will only notice without judgment. Take a slow, deep breath keeping the focus on the breath, and as you inhale, imagine drawing your breath up from the palms of your hands. As you exhale, imagine catching the breath with the palms of your hands, as if your breath is a ball tossed between your hands and your center. Remind yourself of your intention to notice without judgment. Bring your awareness back to your breath as you continue to inhale, drawing breath and energy up from the palms of your hands to the center of yourself, and while exhaling catch the breath with the palms of your hands. Go back and forth between your intention and your breath. Try it for about a minute, and then write down your observations.

This is a brief experience in the present moment, being aware of your breath and the play of energy from your hands and your mind. If you had any difficulty with this exercise, it is important to remember that mindfulness improves with practice.

Moving on to Chapter Four

You now have an introduction to the essential components of TAB: the meridian gateway, mindfulness, touch, breath, intention, and intuition. These tools will help you when you use them with the basic TAB procedural steps we give you in the next chapter.

Chapter 4

The Steps of Basic TAB

Think of TAB as having different levels like a video game. You will first gain some proficiency with the fundamental skills and in future chapters build on what you learn so you become even more self-aware and expand your options for change. In this chapter, you will study basic TAB, which includes thinking about your problem, noticing where you feel distress, rating the level of distress, making an affirmation, stating an intention, locating the meridian treatment sites, doing a brain integration sequence and an eye-roll exercise to strengthen your result. First we begin with some background information and then end with a case example to help clarify the steps. In Chapter 5 you will be able to practice the procedure and work on your problem.

TAB Background

When you do TAB, you Touch and Breathe on selected meridian points, do a brain integration sequence, and Touch and Breathe on the meridian points again. What distinguishes TAB from other meridian-based therapies such as thought field therapy (TFT) or emotional freedom techniques (EFT), which both use similar treatment points, is that you Touch and Breathe on treatment points rather than tap. What also sets TAB apart from evolving thought field therapy (EvTFT) is the use of generic preparation and sequences before a personalized approach to selecting treatments points is learned.

Treatment Point Sequence

There are two different ways to select treatment points. The first is to pick treatment points by way of a personalized method using applied kinesiology (AK) or energy testing (see Chapter 6), and the second is to use a generic sequence.

Personalized Sequence

In the mid-1980s psychologist Roger Callahan (1985) described a treatment for phobias that consisted of patients tapping certain meridian points and doing a series of brain exercises while thinking about their phobias. He showed that you could eliminate the phobia, at times within seconds, and called his treatment thought field therapy (TFT) and trademarked it as the Callahan Techniques. By using applied kinesiology, Dr. Callahan was able to pinpoint the exact order to tap these points.

Dr. Callahan said that points needed to be treated in a certain sequence, much like numbers in a combination lock that need to be in the correct order to open it (Callahan & Callahan, 1996). He also maintained that you could include other points between the correct ones and that the extra points did not interfere with the success of the therapy. For example, unlike a combination lock with the numbers 1, 2, 3 (which would need 1, 2, 3 in that order to open the lock), you could have an effective energy treatment with 8162973 because 1, 2, 3 is in proper order within the sequence 8162973.

Furthermore, as Dr. Callahan used applied kinesiology to develop personal sequences for his patients, he noticed certain patterns of treatment points would come up for a particular problem. He called these patterns of points *algorithms* and decided to try to treat other patients with similar problems with an algorithm rather than a personal sequence. For example, many of his patients with phobias had a pattern of stomach, spleen, and collarbone treatment points that required attention. He then used stomach, spleen and collarbone treatment points for new patients who came in with phobias and he found the recipe effective. Dr. Callahan reported the method was not only successful, but also there were no adverse effects to the treatment because you either had positive results or nothing happened at all.

Generic Sequence

In the late 1980s, after reading Dr. Callahan's book *The Five-Minute Phobia Cure*, psychologist Patricia Carrington began to experiment by tapping on all of the meridian points, rather than limiting the tapping to the points on the specific algorithms that Dr. Callahan developed. She called her treatment *Acutap*, and reported great success with it. With twenty years of recorded cases and documentation, Dr. Carrington (personal communication, April 2007) states that the majority of phobias cleared with tapping. Perhaps more importantly, they did not return.

By the mid-1990s engineer Gary Craig, after studying with Dr. Callahan, also came to the same conclusion that one could treat all of the meridian points and successfully eliminate most, if not all, psychological difficulties a person was having. Gary Craig named his all-purpose technique Emotional Freedom Techniques (EFT), and with the desire to make these methods available to the general public, he launched an intensive Internet campaign to teach these methods to both professionals and the public alike. His e-mail newsletters currently reach over 300,000 readers and there are many professionals using EFT with their clients due to his tireless efforts to make these methods available to all. Throughout the world, there are hundreds of thousands of people using one basic sequence with success.

Overview of Basic TAB Procedure

The TAB basic sequence takes the techniques taught by Callahan Techniques, algorithms, EFT, Acutap and EvTFT and provides you with a mindful, gentle self-help tool.

Meridian Treatment Points

Treatment points are the specific locations on the meridians that you will gently *activate* by Touch and Breathe (TAB). When you locate a treatment point, touch it using the palm side of two or three fingers unless instructed otherwise. You will then concentrate with your intention and your breath as you touch the meridian. Finally, you will focus the energy of your mind, which includes your heart, brain and every cell of your body.

Hand Position

Mindfully position the palm side of your fingers on the meridian treatment points as you learn them, with your palms open, so they act as antennas to your mind's energy and focus the energy on the intended point. Use illustration 4.1 to see where the focus of your intention should be. When touching points on the hand, hold your hands open again as antennas to bring the energy to the meridian point. You will see that many of the treatment points are bilateral, which means they occur on both sides of the body. Although it is not necessary, we encourage you to treat both sides whenever possible.

You may or may not feel something when you Touch and Breathe on meridian points; some people are sensitive to energy, but many are not. You do not need to feel the energy for TAB to work. That being said, you may notice that you want to stay longer on a point, or may feel as though something is shifting or moving within you and we encourage you to notice without judging.

Brain Integration Sequence

In Chapter 1 you read about the brain's plasticity and how your thought processes can actually change your physical brain. TAB includes a sequence of steps (which are similar to Dr. Callahan's brain exercises mentioned earlier) that are thought to exercise or stimulate each part of your brain so that you are in better shape to integrate new information. The steps make up what is known as the integration sequence (Diepold, Britt & Bender, 2004).

When Do You Use the Integration Sequence?

The treatment sequence is always done twice. The integration sequence is between the treatment sequence and the repeated treatment sequence. Similar to a sandwich the treatment sequence is like the two slices of bread and the integration sequence is the filler between the slices.

The Eye-Roll Treatment

There is a calming effect when you look down at the ground and slowly move your eyes from the ground to the sky without moving your head. This visual movement is used in hypnosis as a way to put subjects into trance. In TAB, this way of rolling your eyes is called the *eye-roll*, and is used to reinforce the effects of self-treating with TAB (Diepold, Britt & Bender, 2004). The eye-roll can also be used as a stand-alone technique for rapid relaxation.

When to Use the Eye-Roll?

Although the eye-roll can be used at any point as a means of stress reduction, you will find it especially helpful toward the end of treatment when the SUD or SUE level is down to a two or lower. It will then reinforce the treatment.

Outline of TAB Procedure

The following is a brief outline of the steps that you will learn in greater detail further on in this chapter and then practice using it in the next chapter as you work on a particular problem. The sequence of fourteen treatment points will be given as text, illustration and pictures. You can also go to www.energyofbelief.com for additional support.

1. Think about your problem, fear, or belief.
2. Notice any signs of distress in your body.

3. Rate your level of distress on a zero to ten SUD scale. Rate your level of enjoyment knowing that it is not good for you, or someone you care about, on a zero to ten SUE scale.

4. Rub the neurolymphatic reflex (NLR) (See Illustration 4.1, p. 79 and Pictures 4.1 and 4.2) and make an affirmation.

5. State an intention for change as you touch the side of your hand.

6. Touch and Breathe on a sequence of meridian points.

7. Do the brain integration sequence.

8. Touch and Breathe once again on the same sequence of meridian points.

9. Check your SUD and SUE levels. If two or less go to step sixteen. If more than two go to step ten.

10. Rub the NLR and make an affirmation with "complete" in the wording.

11. State an intention for "complete" change as you touch the side of your hand.

12. Touch and Breathe on a sequence of meridian points

13. Do the brain integration sequence.

14. Touch and Breathe once again on the same sequence of meridian points.

15. Check your SUD and SUE levels. If two or less go to step sixteen. If your SUD or SUE got worse, or is more than two:

    Check: Did my thought or emotion change: (e.g., I started by feeling afraid and I am now angry?) If so, go all the way back to Step 1 and start again with the new thought or emotion.

    Check: Did the SUD or SUE go down several points, but isn't completely eliminated? If so, go to Step 10, inserting the word ***completely*** once again into the affirmation and intention.

16. When your SUD or SUE is two or less, do the eye-roll technique.

17. Check your SUD and SUE levels.

Detailed Instructions for Each TAB Step

The following are each of the seventeen steps in more detail and accompanied by illustrations. Always drink some water before you get started because energy work requires you to be well hydrated. You may also want to massage your neck and shoulders in preparation for your work.

Step 1: Think About Your Problem (Attune Your Problem)

When you are doing TAB, it is best to begin by breaking your problem into small segments. For example: if your problem involves a fear that keeps you from performing normal life activities like driving on highways, think of the different times this fear has interfered with your life. Pick one aspect of the problem, such as the first time you had a problem with the fear, or the worst situation involving the fear. You can later attune another aspect and work on that.

Step 2: Notice Any Signs of Distress

Notice your body. Is your stomach tight, is your heart racing? Do you want to fight or run away and hide?

Step 3: Rate Your SUD and SUE Levels

Using the SUD and SUE scales from Chapter 2, you will first rate your level of distress on a scale of zero to ten. If applicable, you will also rate your level of enjoyment (even though the situation is not good for you or your loved ones) on a scale of zero to ten. Remember, sometimes even destructive behavior has a level of enjoyment. For example, though you may very much want to quit smoking cigarettes or stop overeating, there is a component of enjoyment and relaxation found in these behaviors. We will treat the enjoyment component of the problem with TAB as well as accompanying anxieties and discomfort. If you are unable to get a distress level, you may want to just guess since there are no wrong answers. You may also simply proceed with the self-treatment and notice later, if you are again in the troubling situation, whether your

nproved. In addition, in Chapter 6, we will give you self-test-
_g ...methods to help you determine your distress level.

Step 4: Rub the NLR and Make an Affirmation

In TAB you will use language to acknowledge your position through affirmations made while rubbing the neurolymphatic reflex (NLR) areas.

The NLR can be found on the left side over the breast, several inches below the collarbone (clavicle) and in line with the nipple. (See Picture 4.1)

You may find the spot a bit sore which is normal.

Picture 4.1
Locating the NLR on Left Side of Chest

On the right side, simply duplicate the process using your left hand. In TAB you simultaneously rub the area beneath your hands with deep pressure. (See Picture 4.2)

Picture 4.2
Rubbing the NLR Both Sides of Chest

When you rub the NLR in TAB, you may rub one side (the left) or both sides. When you rub both sides you can either cross your hands or rub the left side with the left hand and the right side with the right hand, although, for most people, rubbing both sides with hands crossed is most effective, some prefer one of the other two methods.

Make an affirmation three times.

Affirmation Statement

As discussed in the last chapter, an affirmation is a statement of acceptance of where you are in the process. In TAB, you may also include some perspective on where the problem is in respect to your history and to your relationship to others who are important to you. It, therefore, can include a statement that recognizes the roots, the causes, the meaning and the problem's impact on others. Make a statement with the following formula: *I accept myself even though I have this problem, fear or belief (its roots, causes, and all that it means and does to me or to others).* (Affirmations will be discussed further in Chapter 8.)

Step 5: State an Intention at the Side of Your Hand

In TAB you will touch the side of your hand when you make a statement of intention. (See Pictures 4.3 and 4.4)

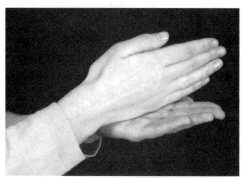

Picture 4.3
Stating Intention at Side of Hand

Intentions will also be discussed further in Chapter 8. For now you just need to use an "I" statement that connects you to your goal. A simple formula is:

I choose, I am ready, I intend

to

give up/let go of/release

(state the problem)

[add the following]

and its roots, causes, and all it means and does to me or to others.

Examples: Fear of flying — *I am ready to let go of my fear of flying in a plane, its roots, its causes, and all that it means and does to me.* Or, stopping a bad habit, — *I am choosing to give up (name the bad habit) its roots, its cause and all that it means and does to me even though I enjoy it because I know it is a problem for those I love.* Or, a negative self-belief such as I'm stupid — *I am intending to let go of my problem belief that I am stupid, its roots, its cause and all that it means and does to me.*

There is no limit to how you can express what your goal is. Notice you can use or decide not to use the statement, "its roots, its causes, and all that it means and does to me." You can say, "its roots, its causes, and all that it means and does to others" especially when your problem impacts the ones you love. (See Picture 4.4)

Picture 4.4
Mindful TAB for Focused Intention

Step 6: Mindfully Touch and Breathe on Each of the Fourteen Meridian Points

There are numerous meridian points. The points used in TAB are the ones generally used by professionals who are working in energy psychology. Touch each of the meridian points while mindfully taking a full respiration, or as many breaths as you choose on each of the twelve meridian points and two vessels described and pictured below. We will show you how to locate each of the treatment points with photos, verbal descriptions and line illustrations. You can also view the points at www.energyofbelief.com.

We recommend you treat both sides of points that are bilateral. Illustration 4.1 shows all fourteen points and the NLR (sore spots). Note that Navel is shown only for mapping purposes and is not used in TAB.

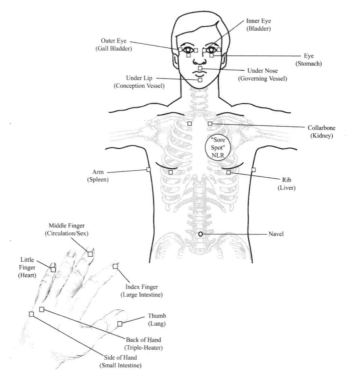

Illustration 4.1

The Fourteen TAB Points

Fourteen TAB Points

As you place your fingers over the points focus on your breath and bringing your attention to the center of the area you are touching. Remember to use your palms as antennae to the energy. Use Illustration 4.1 to pinpoint the area with your intention.

Bladder (BL-1) or inner eye (ie) the inner-most edge of the eye by the bridge of the nose. (Bilateral.) (See Picture 4.5)

Picture 4.5
Inner Eye Treatment Point

Gall Bladder (GB-1) or outer eye (oe*)* — outside corner of the eye in the hollow (depression) on the outer side of the bony part of the eye socket. It is in the hollow and not on the bone. (Bilateral.)

(See Picture 4.6)

Picture 4.6
Outer Eye Treatment Point

Stomach (ST-1) or eye (e) — the center of the lower eye socket (lower side of the bony part), directly below the pupil when you are looking straight ahead. (If you rub that spot lightly, you will feel a tiny notch where the treatment point is located.) (Bilateral.)

(See Picture 4.7)

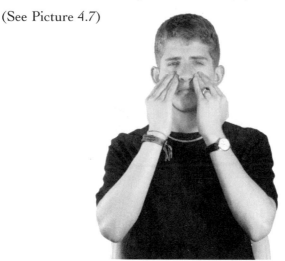

Picture 4.7
Under Eye Treatment Point

Governing Vessel (GV-27) or under nose (un) — center point between the upper lip and the nose. (Not bilateral.) (See Picture 4.8)

Picture 4.8
Under Nose

Conception Vessel (CV-24) or under lip (ul*)* — center of the face in the depression between the lower lip and the chin. (Not bilateral.) (See Picture 4.9)

Picture 4.9
Under Lip Treatment Point

Spleen/Pancreas (SP-21) or arm (a) — about four inches below the armpit. Place four fingers of your hand flat under your arm with the index finger starting at the lower edge of the arm hollow and the pinky toward the ground. You will be in the correct area. (Bilateral.) (See Picture 4.10)

Picture 4.10
Under Arm Treatment Point

Liver (LV-14) or rib (r) — upper edge of the eighth rib, directly below the nipple. May be tender to the touch. (Bilateral.)

(See Picture 4.11)

Picture 4.11
Rib Treatment Point

Lung (LU-11) or thumb (t) — inside corner of the thumbnail. (Bilateral.) (See Picture 4.12)

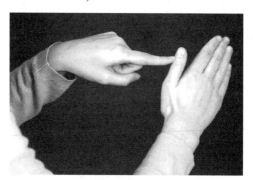

Picture 4.12
Thumb Treatment Point

Large Intestine (LI-1) or index finger (if) — inside corner of the index finger nail. (Bilateral.) (See Picture 4.13)

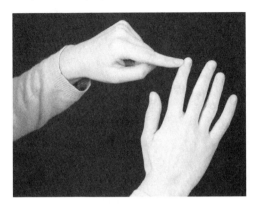

Picture 4.13
Index Finger Treatment Point

Circulation/Sex (CX-9) or middle finger (mf) — inside corner of the middle finger. (This meridian, which deals with the blood circulatory system and the sex organs, is also known as the pericardium meridian.) (Bilateral.) (See Picture 4.14)

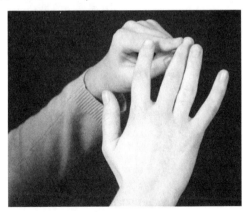

Picture 4.14
Middle Finger Treatment Point

Heart (HT-9) or little finger (lf) — inside corner of the little finger-nail. (Bilateral.) (See Picture 4.15)

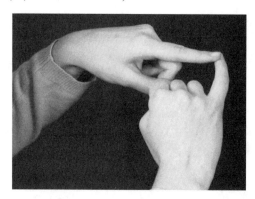

Picture 4.15
Little Finger Treatment Point

Triple Heater (TH-3) or back of hand (bh) — the back of your hand spot can be found on the back of the hand in the slight hollow between the ring and pinky fingers. (The triple-heater is also called the triple-warmer or thyroid meridian). (Bilateral.) (See Picture 4.16)

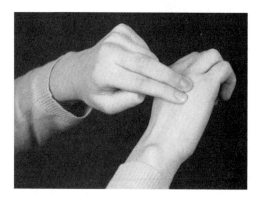

Picture 4.16
Back of Hand Treatment Point

Small Intestine (SI-3) or side of hand (sh) — outer edge of the hand (karate chop side) at the topmost, large crease created when a fist is made. (Bilateral.) (See Picture 4.17 and also Picture 4.4)

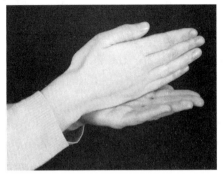

Picture 4.17
Side of Hand Treatment Point

Kidney (K-27) or collarbone (c) — the hollow (depression) where the first rib, clavicle (collarbone) and sternum (breastbone) meet. It is approximately one thumb-width down and one thumb-width over from the suprasternal notch (the v shape place on the top and center of your sternum where it joins your neck.) You can locate this point by putting your fingers under your collarbone and moving them along the bottom of the collarbone until you reach an indentation just below the bony suprasternal notch. (Bilateral.) (See Picture 4.18)

Picture 4.18
Collarbone Treatment Points

Step 7: Do the Brain Integration Sequence

The integration sequence is always done immediately after you have completed a treatment sequence and takes about thirty seconds.

What Does the Integration Sequence Do?

The integration sequence is thought to be a way to exercise the various parts of your brain and activate the brain in a way that is helpful for integrating the effects of TAB on the meridian system. There are various positions in which you focus your eyes in this sequence while touching your collarbone treatment points and your back-of-hand (triple heater) treatment point; this is thought to increase flow of chi throughout the meridian system. Try bringing your awareness to each of the integration sequence steps. For example when you hum, count and hum again to activate the left and right sides of your brain, tune into how your voice humming or speaking resonates in your body. You may find yourself smiling as you hum. When you stimulate your brain in this way, it is thought to be like doing a mental workout at the local brain gym.

Integration Sequence Steps

Begin by using one hand to touch both collarbone treatment points at the same time. Do this by using the tip of your thumb on one point and the tips of your index, middle, and ring fingers on the other point. Next with your other hand, use your index, middle and ring fingers to touch the back-of-hand treatment spot of the hand on your collarbone points. (See Picture 4.19)

Picture 4.19
Hand Position for Integration Sequence

While holding these points, take one full respiration and as you take in your breath, allow the energy of your mind to be drawn to the points in a mindful manner. Then breathing normally, continue to touch the treatment points, trying to keep your head still as you move your eyes in the following steps:

1. Close eyes

2. Open eyes

3. Eyes look down to the right

4. Eyes look down to the left

5. Rotate the eyes in one full circle

6. Rotate the eyes in one full circle in the other direction

7. Hum a tune (for approximately five to seven seconds)

8. Count from one to five

9. Hum a tune again (for approximately five to seven seconds)

Step 8: Repeat the Treatment Sequence

The integration sequence is always followed by the treatment sequence. With mindfulness, take a full respiration and Touch and Breathe on each of the meridian points once again. Take as many breaths as you need at each point.

Step 9: Check Your Work by Rating Your SUD and SUE Levels

Try to go back to the original thought field in order to check your SUD or SUE (because the SUD or SUE is an assessment of that particular thought field) and notice your distress or enjoyment level.

If your SUD and SUE are two or lower go to Step 16, the eye-roll procedure. If your SUD and SUE are more than two go to Step 10.

Step 10: Rub the NLR and Make an Affirmation with "Complete" in the Wording

Your SUD or SUE level may be more than two because your work is incomplete or you have shifted thought fields. Shifting thought fields means you are thinking about (attuning) the problem a little differently than when you started. Sometimes your problem feels worse, because you got more fully in touch with your distress or are thinking about another part of the larger problem. An example of attuning another part of the problem would be that you didn't get a promotion so you decided to attune to your boss giving you the news. Then the thought shifted to seeing the look on your significant other's face when you came home and talked about your failed promotion. A second example would be your decision to try to eat differently: at first, your attuned thought might be about not eating the appetizers at a dinner party and then it shifted to trying to pass up dessert from the elaborate dessert tray.

Sometimes it may be that you are not ready to work on the problem. You will learn how to check this further in Chapter 6 where you learn to self-test.

No matter what the reason, it is important to always acknowledge and accept the results of where you are in your work with an affirmation while rubbing the NLR.

Make an Affirmation
Accepting that Your Self-Work is Incomplete

Rub the NLR and make an affirmation accepting yourself even though your work is not complete. Affirmation formula: *I accept myself even though I am not completely over this problem (its roots, causes, and all that it means and does to me).* Or if you shifted thought fields: *I accept myself even though (state whatever the new thought field is)* — e.g., *I am now angry about what happened.*

Step 11: State an Intention for "Complete" Change

State an intention for "complete" change as you touch the side of your hand. Sometimes a part of you may have concerns about what is happening. You will learn more about this in Chapters 8 and 9. In order to help focus your intention in these situations, you can make the following "I" statement as a start.

I am ready/choosing to be completely over this problem (state the problem) (its roots, causes, and all that it means and does to me).

Step 12: Mindfully Touch and Breathe on Each of the Fourteen Points

Step 13: Do the Brain Integration Sequence

Step 14: Repeat the Treatment Sequence

Mindfully Touch and Breathe on each of the fourteen points.

Step 15: Check Your SUD and SUE Levels

If SUD and SUE are two or less, go to Step 16. If more than two go back to Step 10 and repeat Steps 10 to 15. When your SUD and SUE become less than two go on to Step 16. You may do this repetition as many times as necessary; however it may be more helpful after three or four tries to read the next group of chapters to learn additional skills to treat your problem. In particular, Chapter 7 discusses two important energetic components: polarity and neurological disorganization, which might be impacting your overall health and treatment success.

Step 16: End of Treatment Eye-Roll

At the end of your work you will finish with the eye-roll technique described and pictured below.

Steps for Eye-Roll Treatment

Using the same hand position as the integration sequence, begin by using one hand to touch both collarbone treatment points at the same time.

Do this by using the tip of your thumb on one point and tips of your index, middle and ring fingers on the other point. Next with your other hand, use your index, middle and ring fingers to touch the back-of-hand treatment spot of the hand touching your collarbone points. (See Picture 4.20)

Picture 4.20
Hand Position for Eye-Roll

- Take one full respiration allowing the energy of your mind to be drawn to the points.

- While maintaining contact with the treatment points:

  o Close your eyes.

  o Open your eyes.

  o Looking straight ahead, drop your eyes to the ground and slowly roll your eyes up to the sky taking five to seven seconds. At the top (the sky or ceiling), relax back to a comfortable position.

- Try it.

Step 17: Check Your SUD and SUE Levels

After the eye-roll, your SUD and SUE level should be at zero.

The following example can help you walk through the steps using someone else's experience as a guide.

Jacklyn's Self-Treatment

Jacklyn is a 31-year-old special education teacher whose husband wants them to start a family, but she feels undecided about bringing a child into the world. She describes her own childhood as very painful, as her father left her mother shortly after her birth; her mother was unhappy, and blamed Jacklyn for her dad leaving.

Jacklyn likes being married, and also enjoys the freedom of being able to come and go as she pleases. When she wrote down her fears about having a child, she felt that her biggest fear was that her husband would leave, just like her dad did.

She decided to use TAB to release the distress about having a child. As she thought about having a child, her SUD level was a seven, and she felt a tightness in her chest. She rubbed the NLR and made her affirmation, "I accept myself, even though I am afraid that if I have a child my husband will leave and I will end up like my mother." She used TAB at the side-of-hand and stated her intention, "I am choosing to let go of my fear that if I have a child my husband will leave and I will end up like my mother." She used TAB on all the meridian treatment points, did the integration sequence, and then used TAB on all the meridian treatment points again. When she checked her SUD level, she reported it was worse. It was a ten, and her fists and shoulders were tight, as if she would like to punch someone. She felt really angry about all the abuse and blame she suffered believing that her father's leaving was her fault. She was shocked at the intensity of her anger. "You know, I don't think I ever allowed myself to feel that," she stated.

Jacklyn didn't want to stay stuck in that place. She rubbed the NLR and changed her affirmation to: "I accept myself even though I am furious about what happened." She TABbed at the side of hand and changed her intention to: "I am choosing to release this anger; I don't want it blocking my choices today." She used TAB on all the meridian points again, then the integration sequence; she then used TAB on all the points. The anger lowered to a four, so she rubbed her NLR and made her affirmation "I accept myself even though I am having a hard time completely letting go of my anger," used TAB on the side of hand and her intention became: "I am choosing to completely release this anger." She repeated the treatment by using TAB on all the meridians, then the integration sequence, then TAB on all the meridians again. Her SUD level went to a two, so she used an eye-roll treatment to release what was left. She now felt calm and clear, as if the past was not interfering in her current decision.

Moving on to Chapter Five

In this chapter you have learned all there is about basic TAB, and so you will put it all together in the next chapter and work on a problem of your own.

CHAPTER 5

Basic TAB Practice

I n this chapter you will choose a problem you want to work on and use TAB to clear the issue from your energy field. Follow the steps one at a time and feel free to refer to the previous chapter for clarification.

Exercise: Basic TAB

Start by getting comfortable, drink some water, and massage your neck and shoulders. Think about your problem and notice the area/s of your body that is/are involved. Get a SUD and SUE level, make an affirmation, state an intention, treat the fourteen points, do the integration sequence, and then treat the fourteen points again. End with an eye-roll.

Step 1: Think About Your Problem
(Attune Your Thought Field)

Pick a problem area, memory, fear, behavior pattern, belief, or thought on which you would like to work. Tune into one segment of the problem.

Step 2: Notice any Signs of Distress in Your Body

Focus your mind on the amount of distress the problem causes you in the present moment by scanning for any tension or disturbance in your body. If your problem has an element of enjoyment, focus your mind on the enjoyment and notice any areas of your body where you feel the enjoyment.

My body sensations _____

Step 3: Rate Your Distress with SUD and SUE Levels

SUD

Rate the amount of distress you are experiencing on a scale from zero to ten where zero is no distress and ten is the worst you could experience. (Use the SUD scale in Chapter 2.)

My SUD level is _____

SUE

Rate the amount of enjoyment you are experiencing. Be sure to make the rating including the part of the thought that you know is not good for you, or causes grief for those you love. On a scale from zero to ten where zero is no enjoyment and ten is the most enjoyment you could experience, how much enjoyment do you experience even though you know it is at the cost of your health or a family member's well-being. (Use the SUE scale in Chapter 2.) Remember the important fact about SUE is the amount of enjoyment, even though it is not good for you.

My SUE level is _____

If you have both SUD and SUE levels, work on the distress (SUD) first. Once SUD level is low, work on the enjoyment (SUE).

Step 4: Rub the NLR and Make an Affirmation

a. Crossing your hands over your chest, rub using deep pressure with your fingers on the area beneath your hands. You may find the spot a bit sore, which is normal.

b. State an affirmation three times.

Picture 5.1
Rubbing NLR

I accept myself even though (state the problem, belief, fear) _____
_____ *(its roots, causes, and all that it means and does to me and those I love).*

Step 5: State an Intention at the Side of Your Hand

State an intention for change as you touch the side of your hand and take a deep breath through your nose. (See Picture 5.2)

Picture 5.2
Side of Hand

While touching the side of the hand meridian spot, state an intention: *I am ready/choosing to release this belief/fear/problem* _____

_____

(its roots, causes, and all that it means and does to me an those I love.)

(Do this three times.)

Step 6: Mindfully Touch and Breathe on Each of the Fourteen Meridian Points

Think about your problem. Touch each meridian treatment point and take a deep breath through your nose, in and out at each point. You may take as many breaths as you like before moving on to the next point. (Use Illustration 5.1 as your guide. Reminder: Although shown, the navel is not used in TAB.)

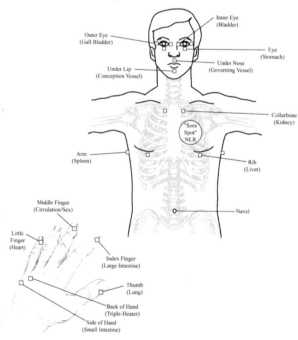

Illustration 5.1
TAB Treatment Point Locations

The basic sequence is as follows:

1. Inner Eye
2. Outer Eye
3. Under Eye
4. Under Nose
5. Under Lip
6. Under Arm
7. Rib/Under Breast
8. Thumb
9. Index Finger
10. Middle Finger
11. Little Finger
12. Back of hand
13. Side of hand
14. Collarbone

Step 7: Do the Brain Integration Sequence

Touch both collarbone treatment points at the same time using the tip of your thumb on one point and tips of your index, middle and ring fingers on the other point. With your other hand, use your index, middle and ring fingers to touch the back of hand treatment spot of the hand on your collarbone points. (See Picture 5.3)

Picture 5.3
Hand Position for Integration Sequence

1. Close eyes

2. Open eyes

3. Eyes look down to the right

4. Eyes look down to the left

5. Rotate the eyes in one full circle

6. Rotate the eyes in one full circle in the other direction

7. Hum a tune (for approximately five to seven seconds)

8. Count from one to five

9. Hum a tune again (for approximately five to seven seconds)

Step 8: Repeat the Treatment Sequence

Touch each of the fourteen meridian treatment points again, taking as many deep breaths at each point as you feel necessary.

The basic sequence is as follows:

1. Inner Eye

2. Outer Eye

3. Under Eye

4. Under Nose

5. Under Lip

6. Under Arm

7. Rib/Under Breast

8. Thumb

9. Index Finger

10. Middle Finger

11. Little Finger

12. Back of hand

13. Side of hand

14. Collarbone

Step 9: Check Your Work by Rating Your SUD and SUE Levels

Focus on your problem area again.

Rate your distress on a scale from zero to ten. Did it get better, worse, or stay the same? Rate your SUE in the same way.

My SUD is _____ *My SUE is* _____

If your SUD and SUE are two or lower, go to Step 16, the eye-roll procedure. If your SUD and SUE are more than two, go to Step 10.

Step 10: Make an Affirmation Accepting that Your Self-Work is Incomplete

Affirmation formula: *I accept myself even though I am not **completely** over this problem (its roots, causes, and all that it means and does to me and others).*

Note: If you have changed to a different thought or emotion, just repeat the treatment steps for the new problem or emotion. Start by accepting where you are now, "*I accept myself even though I have this problem/fear/belief.*" Go back to Step 1 and treat this new problem. Be sure to check your work on your initial problem, and then again with this new problem later.

Step 11: State an Intention for "Complete" Change

State an intention for "complete" change as you touch the side of your hand. (See Picture 5.4)

*I am ready/choosing to be **completely** over* _____
_____ *(its roots, causes, and all it means and does to me and those I love).*

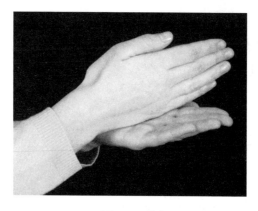

Picture 5.4
Side of Hand

Step 12: Mindfully Touch and Breathe on Each of the Fourteen Points

The basic sequence is as follows:

1. Inner Eye

2. Outer Eye

3. Under Eye

4. Under Nose

5. Under Lip

6. Under Arm

7. Rib/Under Breast

8. Thumb

9. Index Finger

10. Middle Finger

11. Little Finger

12. Back of hand

13. Side of hand

14. Collarbone

Step 13: Do the Brain Integration Sequence

Step 14: Repeat the Treatment Sequence

The basic sequence is as follows:

1. Inner Eye

2. Outer Eye

3. Under Eye

4. Under Nose

5. Under Lip

6. Under Arm

7. Rib/Under Breast

8. Thumb

9. Index Finger

10. Middle Finger

11. Little Finger

12. Back of hand

13. Side of hand

14. Collarbone

Step 15: Check Your SUD and SUE Levels

If your SUD and SUE are two or less, go to Step 16. If more than two, go back to Step 10 and repeat steps ten to fifteen. When your SUD and SUE become two or less, go on to Step 16. You may do this as many times as necessary, but it may be better after three tries to continue reading and find some more individualized ways to get your SUD and SUE lower.

Step 16: End of Treatment Eye-Roll

Touch both collarbone treatment points at the same time with one hand, using the tip of your thumb on one point and tips of your index, middle and ring fingers on the other point. With your other hand, use your index, middle and ring fingers to touch the back-of-hand treatment spot of the hand on your collarbone points. (See Picture 5.5.) It does not matter which hand you use to touch the points. Feel free to use one or you can try alternate hands for the integration sequence and the eye-roll.

Picture 5.5
Hand Position for Eye-Roll

Holding the points, take one full respiration, while drawing your mind energy to the points. Maintain contact with the collarbone points.

Close your eyes. Open your eyes. Keeping your head looking straight ahead, drop your eyes to the ground and slowly roll your eyes up to the sky taking five to seven seconds from ground to sky. Following the eye-roll, relax back to a comfortable position.

Step 17: Check Your Work by Your SUD and SUE Levels

My SUD level is _____ *My SUE level is* _____

Moving on to Chapter Six

Now congratulate yourself for the good work you've done so far! You've now learned the basics of TAB, but there is more. Next we will teach you about self-testing, which is a remarkable way for you to get answers from questions you ask yourself. You will learn to use your energy feedback system as a means of self-communication. This will increase your self-awareness and strengthen your intuitive capacities.

CHAPTER 6

Self-Communication:
Using Your Energy Feedback System

*J*eremy, a 180-pound man, and his wife, Julia, a 120-pound woman, were taking one of Costa Rica's famous eco-tours, in which they happily went white-water rafting and hiking through the jungle. The highlight of their trip was to be the "canopy tour" during which they were to rappel 80 feet up centuries-old cottonwood trees, swing from tree to tree by means of a hook line and get a monkey's eye view of the jungle. After some instruction, Jeremy volunteered to go first. About twenty-five feet up in the air, his muscles weakened and he found that he could not summon the energy to go up or down. Jeremy was at a wall. He was rescued from his frozen position by one of the guides. When he was safely back on solid ground, he told Julia that the climb was far too rigorous for her and that she would not be strong enough to make it either. Julia decided to try it anyway and quickly and easily rappelled up the eighty feet with delight.

What was the difference between Jeremy's and Julia's abilities to meet the challenges of the climb? Both wanted to go up the tree. Both intended to climb and have a good time. Jeremy was clearly bigger and stronger than Julia, but Jeremy was afraid of heights and Julia was not. Jeremy tried to climb despite his fears, but his muscles weakened and he was immobilized, whereas, Julia's muscles were strengthened by her enthusiasm. The phenomena of instantaneous connections of mind-body

— and the weakened or strengthened muscles that result — continue to baffle science. One thing is certain; the answer does not lie simply in the traditional ideas about positive versus negative thinking.

Despite the confusion, some clinical professionals have drawn on this relation of the mind-body energy to help identify certain health issues and to promote physical and emotional well-being. In this chapter you will learn the background and advancements that led to the methods that you will be mastering in order to gain feedback from your own energy system. You will also learn how the influence and confluence of Eastern and Western medicine on one another have led to new ways of treating psychological problems. We teach you three self-tests to gain feedback from your own mind-body-energy system. After practicing the methods, you will then use them to gain further mastery of the two measurement scales SUD and SUE that you have been using since learning them in Chapter 2.

Mind, Muscles and the Human Energy System

In the 1960s, chiropractor George Goodheart developed *Applied Kinesiology* (Walther, 1981), a groundbreaking health care system that combined methods from chiropractic, physical therapy and Chinese medicine into a way to diagnose and treat a variety of diseases, both physical and mental. Applied kinesiology focused on muscles and body movement and was one of the first of the Western health care sciences to realize the implications of the mind-body connection in promoting well-being.

Applied Kinesiology and Emotion

Dr. Goodheart generously opened the workshops he gave on applied kinesiology to professionals from other specialties and set the stage for cross-pollination with the science of psychology. Psychiatrist John Diamond and psychologist Roger Callahan both heard about applied kinesiology and were intrigued by one particular aspect of what they learned; the strength of muscles was influenced by emotions and the strength, or loss of strength, could be evaluated through a method of muscle-testing applied to the acupuncture meridian system.

What applied kinesiology and muscle-testing confirm is the correlation of emotion and strength known to the general population. Have you ever said to someone: "Sit down, I have some bad news to tell you"? If you did, it was because you instinctively knew that the response to the news could cause a weakening or even collapse of the muscles supporting the person. Like Jeremy who was weakened by fear while trying to climb the cottonwood tree, people have been observed to physically lose strength upon learning distressing news.

Dr. Diamond and Dr. Callahan took that observation one step further. They conjectured that muscle-testing in conjunction with the meridian system might provide a way not only to identify the presence of an emotional problem, but also a means to provide psychological treatment.

Muscle-Testing

Perhaps you are familiar with muscle-testing through your own experience with chiropractic or physical therapy. If you are unfamiliar with muscle-testing, Picture 6.1 shows a health care professional muscle-testing the deltoid muscle.

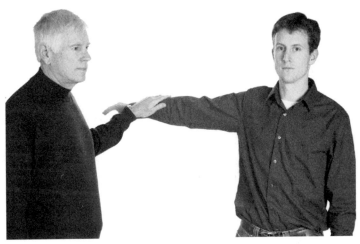

Picture 6.1
Health Care Professional Muscle-Testing

Exploring Your Energy Feedback System

Like the health care professional, who uses energy feedback to guide the course of treatment, you will be able to test and use feedback from your own system to guide self-treatment. Accessing the feedback requires that you study and practice the self-tests in this chapter and apply what you learn in the chapters to follow.

The first step for self-testing is to develop and practice a means of getting reliable responses for **yes/no**, **true/false**, and **positive/negative** questions. The self-tests you will learn are not strictly measures of your body strength since you will see that strength alone does not seem prominent in two of the self-tests. It would be more appropriate to consider them to be responses, which depend on some coordinated mind-body-energy synergy to provide information about your system. The self-test feedback response can give one of three responses. The response can be *yes*, *no*, or *uncertain*. We'll guide you in learning how to read the feedback clearly and consistently.

In the pages that follow, three ways to self-test are described. We recommend you try all of them and see which one works best for you. The art and skill of self-testing will come as you practice and gain experience. You will learn to problem solve using your mind-body-energy connection, and whatever you learn will be what is true or unique for your psychological makeup. Most people experience self-testing as fun, interesting, and even intriguing! You will learn to tune into yourself in a way that perhaps you have never done before.

Please note: As an additional aide you may go to the website www. energyofbelief.com and follow the videotape there demonstrating each of these self-tests.

Tuning into Your Mind-Body-Energy

You will begin by going through the preliminary steps, which you already know from your work in Chapters 4 and 5, to ensure you get the most accurate responses as you self-test. You'll be learning why in the next chapter.

Exercise: Preparation to Ensure Accurate Self-Testing

1. Begin by getting yourself properly hydrated with a full glass of water.

2. Set an *intention* at the side of hand to be able to self-test. *I am ready/choosing to learn to self-test.*

3. Take a full breath, if possible through your nose, and bring your *awareness* into your mind-body. This means notice what's happening inside you. Perhaps it's the beat of your heart, or the sound of your breath, or a feeling of warmth or coolness in your fingertips. Some people, especially those who have a hard time quieting their minds, find it helpful to bring awareness to their feet. You are only noticing without judgment as to right or wrong. You are entering into a state of mindfulness.

4. Now take your hands and massage the back of your neck and shoulders, as if you are giving yourself a neck and shoulder massage.

5. Cross your hands over your chest, and rub the NLR on the front of the chest. (See Picture 6.2, Rubbing NLR.) Remember NLR can be rubbed on one side (the left) or both sides. Try both ways and see which works best for you. It is your choice.

Picture 6.2
Rubbing NLR

Exercise: Connect Your Thoughts, Sensations, and Emotions

Having done the preparation, sit back comfortably in your chair. You may leave your eyes open or closed and then think a pleasant thought. Notice what bodily sensations come with that thought. You might, for example, have comfortable feelings accompanied by a body experience such as the heart beating faster or slower, a feeling in the toes, a change in breathing, or you may not notice much all. There are no right or wrong responses!

Write your pleasant thought here: _____

_____

If you have a feeling and any body experience with the pleasant thought, write your feelings down and where in your body you notice them the most. Write any of your accompanying thoughts, feelings, sensations, sounds, smells, tastes, or images:

_____

_____

Now sit back again, closing your eyes if you so choose. This time think a mildly unpleasant thought and notice any accompanying feelings and how you experience this in your body. You might have uncomfortable feelings accompanied by a body experience such as a tightness or sharpness somewhere in your body, or you may not notice anything different. Again, there are no right or wrong responses! All that matters is that you pay attention to what you feel and experience.

Write your unpleasant thought here: _____
_____

If you have a feeling and any body experience with the unpleasant thought, write your feeling/s and where in your body you notice them. Write down any of your accompanying thoughts, feelings, sensations, sounds, smells, tastes, or images:

_____

_____

Notice how quickly your body can respond to a thought with emotions, sensations, and feelings. Notice also whether your emotions and body sensations change when you go from one thought to another or whether they stay the same. Notice whether you are surprised by any of your responses.

Exercise: Self-Test Sway

Now standing up, repeat the exercise of thinking and notice what happens to your body. First, read through what you will be doing and noticing, then put the book down, stand up, and try it. If you relax while you are doing the following exercise, you will find that your body will tend to sway either backward or forward and notice which way you tend to sway as you do the following exercises. First take a deep breath and bring your awareness to the soles of your feet. Think the same pleasant thought and notice if your body sways forward or backward, and now think the same unpleasant thought and notice which way your body sways. Next, while still standing, think the word **yes** (think **yes,**

yes, yes) and notice whether your body sways forward or backward. Then think the word **no** (think **no, no, no**) and notice in which direction you sway. Last, while still standing, think of something you know is true like "2 + 2 is 4" or "my name is _____" and think your name. Then think of something you know is untrue like "2 + 2 is 7" or "my name is_____" and think a name that is not your own.

Now put this book down and try the exercise before you continue reading.

Circle your results.

Direction of sway for pleasant thought — Circle one: forward or backward

Direction of sway for unpleasant thought — Circle one: forward or backward

Direction of sway for **yes** — Circle one: forward or backward

Direction of sway for **no** — Circle one: forward or backward

Direction of sway for 2 + 2 = 4 — Circle one: forward or backward

Direction of sway for 2 + 2 = 7 — Circle one: forward or backward

For most people, the body will sway forward on a pleasant thought, the word **yes** or something that is true. For most people, the body will sway backward on a negative thought, the word **no** or something that is untrue.

Additional Self-Testing Methods

There are many ways to self-test and thereby set up a means of determining the effects of what you are thinking on your mind-body-energy system and here are two more methods: the first involves using the muscles of your thumb and index finger; the second involves the amount of friction generated by rubbing your thumb and index finger together. Over the years, there have been many creative adaptations of these methods from colleagues and students and you, too, are encouraged to explore other methods for yourself.

As in the sway self-test, you should make statements that reflect the difference between **yes** or **no**, **true** or **false** and **positive** or **negative** in your responses. You can try each way and decide which method works best for you. Some people like to stay with one method and others like to use a few different ones.

Remember, there is no right or wrong response. It is only necessary for you to experience a difference in the self-test between two responses — the response to **yes** must differ from the response to **no**. Under no circumstance is it ever necessary to guess or force a response. Your job is to just notice the differences at a physically comfortable level. Should you doubt the response, do it over again.

Exercise: The Chain Link Method

A. Press the pads of the thumb and index finger of your non-dominant hand tightly together, forming an O-ring shape as shown in Picture 6.3. Link the thumb and index finger of your dominant hand through the O-ring, at the pad of the fingers, creating another O-ring. The result should resemble a chain link.

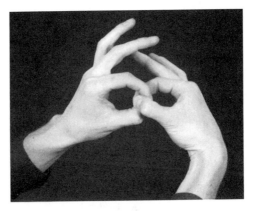

Picture 6.3
Self-Test
Chain Link Method

B. Take a breath and bring awareness to your fingers. Holding the O-ring fingers tightly together, use the two fingers of your dominant hand to try to pull open the O-ring fingers of your nondominant hand. Usually, you will be unable to pull the fingers apart: this will give you a baseline strong response.

C. While you are energy testing with your fingers in this way, notice if you get a strong or weak response to thinking the word **yes** and then thinking the word **no.** Then think **yes/no** and true/false statements like, "Today is Tuesday (correct day of the week)" and, "Today is Friday (incorrect day of the week)" and muscle test. Try it.

When your body energy is flowing properly, the fingers should remain strongly together for truthful statements, and weaken and come apart to false statements.

D. Now think a positive thought and, as you do so, use your dominant O-ring fingers to try to pull open the O-ring fingers of your nondominant hand. The fingers should remain strong or closed. Now, think a negative thought and try again to pull the fingers apart. They should come apart easily.

E. If you are unable to pry the fingers open under any circumstances, then try pressing the thumb and ring finger together to form the O-ring with your nondominant hand. If that does not work, try the pinky finger and the thumb. The fingers are progressively easier to separate as you move towards the pinky finger of your nondominant hand.

Exercise: The Glide Method

A. Place the pads of the thumb and index finger of either hand lightly together, forming a duckbill shape. (See Picture 6.4.) Take a breath and bring your awareness to your fingers. Lightly rub those fingers back and forth against each other. You should have a baseline smooth feeling.

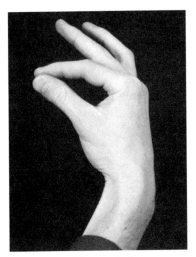

Picture 6.4

Self-Test Glide

The smooth feeling can be described as frictionless or as a glide sensation.

B. Now think the words **yes** and rub your fingers. Think the word **no** and rub your fingers. Then think some **yes/no** and true/false statements like, "Today is Tuesday (correct day of the week)" and "Today is Friday (incorrect day of the week)." Try it.

When your body energy is flowing properly, the fingers should glide smoothly against each other for truthful statements, and feel sticky, rough or stuck in response to false statements.

C. Now think a positive thought and, as you do, lightly glide your fingers back and forth against each other. The fingers should remain smooth as they glide. Now, think a negative thought and glide the fingers against each other again. The fingers should feel some friction like rough, sticky or stuck as you do this.

D. If you are unable to gain a distinction between the two responses try the other hand or another finger with the thumb.

Uses for Self-Tests

You will find self-tests invaluable for a number of reasons in TAB and we will give more suggestions in later chapters. One important way to use a self-test is to check whether you should work on a particular problem or work on something else first. Another way is to check your SUD and SUE levels when you are unsure of them.

Questions about Where to Start Your Self-Work

Sometimes you may be unsure of what part of a problem you want to start working on. You can self-test for some help in making the decisions. Say: *It's okay for me to start on this problem at this time.* Self-test. Then check for the reverse: *It's not okay for me to start on this problem at this time.* Self-test. Or: *There is something else I must work on before I start this problem.* Self-test. Then check for the reverse: *There is nothing else to check before I start to work on this problem.* Self-test.

If you get **no** to *it's okay for me to start on this problem at this time*, then you check for whether or not there is something else that must be done first. Never work on something to which you have received a **no**. Almost always, there is something else that is found to be important to do first.

Self-Test for SUD and SUE Levels

In the last chapter you wrote a number measurement of the level of disturbance and/or elation you had when thinking about your problem. Sometimes you may not be able to give a number to your level of disturbance. If this happens, you can either work without the number or try to get the number by self-testing. If you decide to get the number, tune into the problem and ask yourself some questions that require either a **yes** or a **no**. You then can self-test using any one of the methods suggested above by asking questions that narrow down the number. For example you could ask yourself, *"is my level of distress less than five?"* Self-test. If you get **yes** ask yourself, *"is it less than three?"* If you get **no** ask yourself, "*is it less/more than seven?*" Continue self-testing until you get a **yes** for the exact number.

Exercise: Using the SUD Scale and Self-Test

"*When I think of my problem how upset (disturbed or distressed) am I right now on a scale of zero to ten with zero being **no** disturbance or upset and ten being the highest or worst disturbance possible?*"

Self-Test for number. _____

Exercise: Using the SUE Scale and Self-Test

On a scale of zero to ten, with zero being no enjoyment or neutral, and ten being the highest degree of enjoyment or pleasure I can imagine (even knowing it is not good for me or for others), how great is my enjoyment?

Self-Test for number. _____

Common Questions about Self-Testing

The following are a few questions we are frequently asked about self-testing.

Why the Strong/Smooth and Weak/Rough Responses?

Why our bodies respond one way to pleasant thoughts and memories and differently to unpleasant thoughts and memories evokes a great deal of curiosity. One possible explanation is that when we think of things that are positive, pleasant, and true, our bodies respond in a strong, solid, and effortless fashion. However, when we think of things that are negative, upsetting, and false, our bodies' energy is blocked, disorganized, and weakened as a result. While there may be many possible explanations involving brain activity, biochemical changes, and body energy adjustments, no one has yet established a definite explanation.

Which Method is Best?

See which self-test method works best for you. Make a series of statements that require a **yes** or **no** response — any true/false statement will suffice. The following are some statements routinely used:

- Say your correct name using the following format: *"My name is …"* Test your response to your statement using any or all of the self-test exercises on the previous pages. The self-test should result in a **yes** (forward sway, strong muscle, or smooth glide). Then say a name that is *not* your own (*"My name is…"*) and test that response. The self-test should result in a **no** (backward sway, weak muscle, or a rough/sticky or **no** glide).

- Follow the same format as above. Say, *"2 plus 2 equals 4."* Test your response using any or all of self-tests you found work best for you. The self-test should result in a **yes** (forward sway, strong muscle or smooth glide). Then say, *"2 plus 2 equals 7"* and re-test the response. The self-test should result in a **no** (backward sway, weak muscle or a rough/sticky glide).

What if You Have Difficulty Getting a Difference in Self-Testing?

The most common reasons that you may have difficulty in self-testing are 1) you are not well hydrated; 2) you have disorganized polarity (see Chapter 7), or 3) you are overwhelmed with strong unpleasant thoughts while practicing. If you are someone who thinks a lot and has a hard time quieting your mind, it is especially helpful to follow the instructions to bring your awareness to a neutral area like your feet.

Self-testing is about interfacing the mind-body-energy, so simply staying in your head with only your thoughts, may not allow you to find the deeper part of your knowing. If you have tried the self-test methods and still cannot distinguish between your *yes* or *no* response, go to Chapter 7 and try one or more of the breathing exercises and then try the self-tests again. If you still have no success with self-testing, read Chapters 8 and 9 about blocking beliefs.

In addition, it is helpful to keep away from strong, unpleasant thoughts while practicing. Save those issues for after you become experienced with the method. Although these issues and thoughts are the reasons for you to learn how to self-test and use TAB, you will find it easier to master the concepts of self-testing on more neutral subject matter.

What are the Limits of Self-Testing?

There are safety measures for self-testing which are very important. Like the polygraph or lie detector test, there is fallibility. You should never ask yourself a question that, if answered incorrectly, would endanger your well-being or the well-being of someone else. For example, if you have a suspicion that you were physically abused when you were little but have no real memory of this, it would not be appropriate to self-test around an unverifiable suspicion. You are learning self-testing to get over self-defeating thoughts, beliefs and behaviors that are compromising your life. The method is not intended to help you to go on a witch-hunt or predict the future, nor is it meant to answer the exact circumstances that brought you to a problem. They are methods that will help you connect to yourself in a way that allows you to correct energy disruptions keeping you from healthy goals.

Moving on to Chapter Seven

Now you have taken the first steps toward learning how to use your energy feedback system as a form of self-communication. You may have found it very easy and natural to do, or you may have found that it took practice and patience. However, each time you practice, you will become more tuned into how your mind-body-energy work together.

Next, we teach you how to use self-testing to learn about two very interesting human energy system phenomena: polarity and neurological disorganization. In the next chapter you will learn how your body energy has an expected pattern of flow and we'll also teach you how to check and correct it if necessary.

CHAPTER 7

Polarity and
Neurological Disorganization

In order for TAB to work properly, your energy system must be operating in the correct, natural flowing pattern. These patterns have been described in Eastern healing as energies flowing across the center of the body and moving freely within and outside the body in the proper direction. In this chapter you will learn about two types of energetic problems that you may encounter when doing TAB: polarity and neurological disorganization. We shall define these concepts, offer speculations about their causes, and teach you how to correct them.

Detecting Mind–Body–Energy Problems

Intuitively, you are aware of energetic problems when you experience the inner sense that something is wrong, or when you aren't feeling like yourself. For example, you can't wake up to go to work, even though you have slept the whole night; or you can't get to sleep yet you're totally exhausted; or maybe you forget and misplace things and you feel frazzled and frustrated. Some acupuncturists, Reiki practitioners, craniosacral practitioners, and other bodyworkers and healers can assess energy disruptions by either feeling or seeing your energy patterns. These individuals actually have an interactive experience with the energy and can help you to correct it.

General Polarity Problems

Polarity is the direction of your energy flow. Human energy fields are invisible, but like a magnetic field, they have a normal direction. The forces that determine the flow of energy remain unknown, but some theories suggest it is related to other forces, such as gravity or the flow of polar compounds such as water and oxygen. Although the total picture is complex, you can think of yourself like the planet Earth, with a north and a south pole: the top of your head shows one polarity and the bottom of your feet shows the opposite. When your polarity is correct your energy flows freely.

An overall negative feeling indicates *general polarity* problems and people with general polarity problems often have a multitude of health problems and frequently report that medicine or other treatments don't work for them. For example, they have sores that won't heal, or headaches or body aches that are unrelieved by standard medical treatment. They encounter difficulties in many areas of life and frequently describe their lives as if they "just can't get started." What they describe is like having your batteries in backward. Another sign that your general polarity is disrupted may occur at the beginning of TAB treatment. If your SUD or SUE level does not change at all, you may have a general polarity problem. At that point it is imperative to use the polarity test described below, because to be successful with TAB requires an energy system that flows properly.

There are numerous theories concerning the many causes of general polarity disruption. In general, it is theorized that something you are eating, or an environmental toxin, is often the source. We encourage you to explore some of the resources such as Radomski and Rapp both listed at the back of the book for a more in-depth study of energetic toxins.

Testing for General Polarity Problems

In order to correct any polarity problems, you must first self-test to determine whether you have a problem with your general polarity and then you must correct the problem or you will not be able to do TAB.

Hand-Over-Head Test

The hand-over-head test assesses your general polarity.

Take a full respiration through your nose and bring your awareness to your feet. Hold one of your hands, **palm down** (toward the ground) over your head, several inches above the scalp, and self-test using one of the methods you learned in Chapter 6. (See Picture 7.1)

Picture 7.1
Hand-Over-Head, Palm Down

What is the result of your test? **(yes or no)** _____

Next hold the same hand **palm up** (toward the sky) over your head, the same short distance above the scalp, and self-test again. (See Picture 7.2)

Picture 7.2

Hand-Over-Head, Palm Up

What result do you get now? **(yes** or **no)** _____

Picture 7.3

Example of the Hand-Over-Head with Glide Self-Test

Organized Mind-Body-Energy Polarity

Your general polarity is correctly organized when in the hand-over-head **palm down** test, you self-test **yes;** and in the hand over the head **palm up** test, you self-test **no.** This is the desired result and we call this being *correctly polarized.*

Disorganized General Polarity

If you got the opposite results, **palm down** gave you a **no**, and **palm up** yielded a **yes,** (or both responses were **yes**, or both were **no,** or your response was indistinguishable) you must correct these responses in order to proceed with self-treatment.

Correcting General Polarity Problems

Frequently, a mind-body-energy polarity disruption is caused by a toxin buildup in the body. In order to assist the body to move the toxin, it is helpful to take the following steps:

1. Drink a glass of water.

2. Rub the back of your neck and shoulders as in a neck and shoulder massage. (See Picture 7.4)

3. Rub the NLR areas on the front of your chest. The NLR is on both sides of your body. Although the action seems strongest on the left side above the heart, we have found that crossing your hands in front of the chest and rubbing the NLR spots simultaneously on both sides of the body has generated more thorough results for people who have disorganized polarity, or are feeling sluggish.

4. Check your work. Do the hand-over-head and check if you have corrected the polarity.

Picture 7.4
Rubbing the NLR

Historical Background of the NLR

In the 1930s, Frank Chapman, DO, described neurolymphatic reflexes and associated them with poor lymphatic circulation (Walther, 1988). The lymph system is an integral part of your immune system and since it has no pump, it depends on muscle contraction and massage for movement of the materials that fight dis-ease and the resulting toxic wastes.

Later, Dr. Goodheart (Walther, 1981) experimented with the neurolymphatic reflexes (NLR) and found that when touched (palpated), individual reflexes strengthened in what he found to be related muscles. The guess was that stimulating the NLR area through self-massage helped remove body toxins contributing to observed deficiencies in muscle response. Rubbing or massaging the NLR was analogous to flushing the lymph toilet.

Identifying the Causes of General Polarity Disorganization

When you find your polarity is disrupted, with some detective work you may be able to uncover the source of the difficulty. You can self-test on foods, perfumes, or other things with which you come into contact.

Neurological Disorganization

Neurological disorganization refers to a state in which you feel either foggy or disorganized. For instance, you may have had an experience of mindlessly walking into a room and not remembering why you went in. Similarly, you may have been distracted and unconsciously changed words saying, "Hand me the hammer" when you meant the flashlight. Perhaps your timing was off when playing golf or tennis, or maybe you were clumsier than usual, bumping into corners and dropping things. Again, you might have found yourself stuttering, unable to access the right word, or maybe reversing letters when you were reading or writing. Also, when you are neurologically disorganized, you often fall asleep while reading, or you may read the same paragraph over and over again without remembering what you just read. In addition, if you find yourself panicking, obsessing, or ruminating over problems and just can't seem to figure out a solution, it is likely that you are in this state.

Many external and internal processes can result in neurological disorganization. Some common causes are stress felt at work, being overtired, using a computer or a cell phone for too long, or sitting under fluorescent lights. Whatever the cause, the outcome is usually the same: your actions, thoughts and words become scrambled, which is fundamentally an energetic phenomenon.

Neurological disorganization can also occur naturally when you are trying to learn something new and all you can to do is correct yourself and push the upward limits of what you are learning. Chiropractor Robert Blaich (1988) speculated that the phenomenon of neurologic disorganization naturally occurs in a transformation process whenever the body adjusts to new limits of higher performance, after being pushed beyond its usual comfort zone. In one study Dr. Blaich had students try to learn to read faster and faster and each time students pushed their limits to read even faster, they became disorganized. It seemed that the disorganization was correlated to breathing, so Dr. Blaich had them do breathing exercises. Then the students became reorganized and were able to continue reading at an even faster rate. All the students in the study increased their reading and comprehension speeds.

Identifying Neurological Disorganization

In TAB, neurological disorganization can be recognized by the rate your SUD and SUE lower; it can also be observed through a test designed specifically for that purpose.

SUD and SUE Levels

When you are neurologically organized your SUD and SUE level will decrease quickly working with TAB. For example, you begin at a SUD level of ten when thinking about a problem; then after one round of treatment, the SUD will be a four, and after two more rounds of treatment, you will have eliminated your discomfort.

In contrast, when you are neurologically disorganized your SUD level changes very slowly and the level will go down from a ten only one number at a time. In other words, progress is very slow. If this is the case, use the following technique to identify neurological disorganization.

Testing for Neurological Disorganization

1. Check your overall polarity to make sure that it is correct using the hand-over-head tests.

2. Draw a big X on a piece of paper   X

3. Draw two parallel lines on another piece of paper | |

4. Self-test while looking at the X. Do you get a **yes** or a **no**?

5. Self-test while looking at the parallel lines. Do you get a **yes** or a **no**? _____

6. You are neurologically disorganized if you test **no** on the X and **yes** on the II, or if you get the same response (**yes**, **no** or unreadable) on both of them.

Correcting Neurological Disorganization

There are numerous ways to correct neurological disorganization. Many of them are well known to you, such as getting a good night sleep and daily exercise. Any exercise that involves "crossing over" such as swimming, running, walking with a brisk arm swing, and cross-country skiing will help your energy cross over the midline which, as discussed previously, is part of optimal energy flow. Other quick techniques to cross your energy include drawing the infinity sign, either on paper or by moving your eyes in this pattern, or moving your hands in this pattern in the air, like a dance or a tai chi movement.

Exercises to Correct Neurological Disorganization

To correct neurological disorganization, the following set of exercises has also been found to be helpful. We suggest you practice each with mindfulness, bringing your awareness to the feel and sound of your breath, the feel and sound of your heart, and the resonance of mind and body working together.

Centering

This exercise is a basic yoga technique and is meant to help center yourself, gathering in your energies, and closing your aura. It is also helpful in protecting yourself from other people's negative moods and energy. Repeat this exercise three times.

1. Bring the palms of your hands together to the middle of your chest with thumbs touching the heart. Take one full respiration in this position. (See Picture 7.5)

Picture 7.5
Centering Position One

2. On the next inhalation bring the thumb of your left hand down to the navel and raise your right hand above your head, extending the thumb straight up. (See Picture 7.6)

Picture 7.6
Centering Inhale

3. On the exhalation return the palms of your hands together mid-chest with thumbs touching the heart. (See Picture 7.7)

Picture 7.7
Centering Exhale

4. On the next inhalation, switch hands, bring the thumb of your right hand down to the navel and extend the thumb straight up on your raised left hand. (See Picture 7.8)

Picture 7.8
Centering Inhale Opposite Hand Position

5. On the exhalation return the palms of your hands together to the middle of your chest with thumbs touching the heart. Take one full respiration in this position. (See Picture 7.9)

Picture 7.9
Centering Exhale

Centering: Repeat this exercise three times

Neurologic Organizer Treatment (NOTx)

Another helpful exercise you can use for neurological disorganization is the Neurologic Organizer Treatment. The NOTx is a combination of breathing exercises developed by the BDB Group (Diepold, Britt & Bender, 2004). Dr. Diepold developed it for his wrestling teams and the exercises can easily be done lying on the ground, as well as in the sitting position.

I. Ankle and wrist position

- Place left ankle over right ankle.

- Stretch hands out straight in front of you, back to back. (See Picture 7.10)

Picture 7.10
NOTx Hands Out, Ankles Crossed

- Place right hand over left hand. (See Picture 7.11)

Picture 7.11
NOTx Hands Crossed Opposite to Ankles

- Interlock fingers and fold hands in, and rest knuckles on chest. (See Picture 7.12)

Picture 7.12
NOTx Hands Brought Interlocked to Chest

II. Breathing pattern

- Take three normal respirations through your nose.
- Place tongue tip to roof of mouth, and take one full respiration
- Place tongue tip to floor of mouth, and take one full respiration.
- Relax tongue, and do the following:

  1. Take a FULL breath in and hold (two seconds).
  2. Force more breath in and hold.
  3. Let breath halfway out and hold.
  4. Let breath all the way out and hold.
  5. Force more breath out and hold.
  6. Take a half breath in and hold.
  7. Breathe normally.

- Reverse ankle and hand positions in Part I above.

- Repeat breathing pattern in Part II above.

Overcoming Chronic Energy Disturbances

It is important to distinguish between energy problems that occur chronically from those that occur infrequently. For chronic problems, it is critical to understand that it will take more than just one treatment for your energies to remain working correctly on a consistent basis. We recommend that you self-test on a daily basis (and throughout each day) to determine if the corrections are holding. It has been our experience, and the experience of other energy practitioners, that some energy corrections involve using the above techniques several times per day, for at least thirty days, in order to create a new energy habit. In other cases, it will also involve you investigating the cause of the disruption, and eliminating that from your diet or environment.

Pam's Story

*Pam is a 62-year-old retired history teacher who has felt that her ability to focus and learn in the past five years has declined. She thought it was just "old age." She described how clumsy she had become, and how she would fall asleep when reading. When she self tested on the X test, she tested **no**. She was excited to think that these techniques could possibly help her, and was determined to use these strategies to help her function at her best. She reported that for the first two weeks she did both the centering technique and the NOTx treatment five times a day. By the end of the second week, on several occasions she tested correctly on the X test. She also began to notice how after an hour at the computer her self-test showed she was disorganized again. She began to limit her computer time, and take a quick walk outside if she had to be there for longer than an hour. She noticed her work output actually improved after doing this, because she was more alert and able to focus. By the end of the third week, she was testing positive with increased frequency. She continued with the treatments, and reported that after six weeks she was only occasionally in the state of disorganization, and was able to recognize and treat it immediately. She was so excited about the renewed ability* *to focus, that she joined a yoga class to keep her energies in the optimal direction. Her general health and outlook on life improved dramatically.*

One of the most helpful books to understand and correct energetic disruptions, with numerous illustrations and exercises is the book *Energy Medicine* by Donna Eden and David Feinstein (1998). In particular, you will find that their five-minute energy routine is especially helpful to correct these energetic patterns.

Jet Lag

We will end this chapter with a story about jet lag, the body's reaction to travel across time zones. Many people have energy disruptions when traveling and jet lag can be treated either as disorganized polarity or neurological disorganization. When people suffer from jet lag, they have all the characteristics of both disruptions.

Treating the meridians and keeping your polarity corrected throughout travel across time zones is frequently reported to be helpful. If you have suffered jet lag in the past, use a combination of the treatment methods above every hour while traveling and notice if it makes a difference for you.

Chun Mei's story illustrates how knowing about unavoidable energy disruptions in advance can help. On her outgoing trip, she used one method of treatment, and on the return trip she used the other. She found they were equally successful.

Chun Mei's Story

Chun Mei, a 32-year-old radiologist flew back and forth to China from the United States twice a year to visit her family. She always lost a few days when she arrived in China and then had to take an extra week off from work on her return to the United States because of jet lag. When she checked her polarity after a trip each way, it was locked and her fatigue and disorientation was a ten. She had started psychotherapy for a separate issue, but when she told her psychologist about the jet lag, she was taught to do a correction each hour of her travel that she was awake. On her return session, Chun Mei reported that both trips were the best they'd ever been for her as she had been able to sleep on the plane on the flight over and she managed to be functional during the early part of the vacation without requiring days of adjustment. Following her return trip, instead of needing a week off from work, she recovered in two days. She was thrilled and attributed it strictly to her attention to her corrections during both flights.

Chun Mei treated the polarity on the trip going to China by rubbing the NLR each hour and doing the NOTx. On the return, she went through the fourteen meridian points each hour, did an integration sequence and repeated the points again. In this way she was able to treat the crossing of the time zones problem easily. For her it was an experiment to see if her mind could change her energetic experience of the time zones. This leads us to the subject of the next chapter where we discuss how the energy of negative beliefs can create polarity reversals.

Moving on to Chapter Eight

In this chapter you have learned about general polarity and neurological disruptions and techniques to self-test both of these states. In the next chapter we teach you about the impact of beliefs on your energy system.

CHAPTER 8

The Energetic Impact of Beliefs on Your Intentions

In this chapter we will discuss the energetic effects of thoughts and beliefs on your mind-body-energy system. We will help you identify the impact of these thoughts and beliefs on your intentions to reach your goals and we'll also teach you techniques to uncover thoughts and beliefs beneath your conscious awareness that may be affecting your life. Specifically, we will explore some common blocking beliefs centered on safety, deservedness, relationships, and the future.

The Energetic Influence of Negative Thoughts

Negative thoughts can impact a mind-body-energy system that is functioning correctly. As described in Chapter 7, a correctly functioning mind-body-energy system is one in which your energies test **yes** when you do the hand-over-head, palm down test and test **no** when you do the hand-over-head, palm up test.

When your system is energetically organized and you think of a problem you want to work on, your self-test will be **no** or negative. For example, you might be correctly polarized and neurologically organized talking with someone about your vacation, but when you switch the discussion to your annoying co-worker, your system disorganizes, and you self-test **no**. Think back to the exercises you did when you were learning to self-test in Chapter 6, when you focused on an unpleasant thought, and your system weakened or responded **no**. The following story about James is an example of the effects of thoughts on your energy system.

James's Story

James is a 29-year-old school teacher who has been going through a divorce for the past year and a half. His wife had an affair, which was the event that initiated the divorce; however, he states the marriage was failing long before the affair. Now, a year later, he lives in an apartment and has custody of his two small children three days a week. He reports that he is generally in a good mood now, but inevitably when he hears his wife's name or comes in contact with her, he finds himself getting angry, and making snide comments. He is especially upset that he can't seem to control himself in front of his two small children, and he sees the hurt in their eyes when he talks badly about their mom. He stated, "I wish I didn't lose my sanity every time I hear her name" and his self-test went weak at the mere mention of her name. (We will discuss his treatment later on.)

In TAB, you expect to get a negative self-test when thinking about your problem, because perturbations and elaters in the thought fields are connected to emotions that support unwanted behaviors. When you experience the negative connection, your system becomes weak or disorganized, and you should test **no**. We discussed how to remove the perturbations and negative elaters from thought fields in Chapters 4 and 5, and you will learn more methods in Chapter 10.

In some cases, however, a problem can actually make someone self-test **yes**. In addition, when you self-test on the statement, "I want to be over this problem," the self-test response is **no**. In those cases it is safe to assume that you have a blocking belief, and that your mind-body-energy system is not operating in a free flow. In our clinical experience, we have found that most patients have blocking beliefs that began at a young age. These blocking beliefs often helped them make sense of or cope with the world.

Historical Background
of Thought Field Polarity Disruptions

In studies of the connection between muscle strength and emotions or thoughts, Dr. Roger Callahan and Dr. John Diamond independently observed a rather extraordinary phenomenon. They found that some of their patients were having a very unexpected response to muscle-testing; when thinking about something pleasant, they muscle-tested negative and other times when thinking about something negative, they muscle-tested positive. This is the exact opposite result than would be expected. Dr. Diamond found that when he muscle-tested patients while they were making a statement of positive intention he observed they became weak/**no** on muscle-testing. For example, while stating, "I choose to be over this problem," they tested negatively and while stating "I choose to keep this problem," they had a positive test **yes**. Dr. Diamond believed this unexpected response had broad personal and societal implications and termed the experience a *reversal of body morality*. He theorized that the reversal prevented healing because life-energy was not being properly directed.

Dr. Callahan also observed the same perplexing phenomena and called it *psychological reversal*, defining it as "...a state of the body and the mind that blocks the natural healing (energy) force within and prevents effective therapeutic intervention" (Callahan, 1991, p. 42).

These psychological reversals represent a literal reversal of the self-test. You get **yes** when you would expect **no** and **no** when you would expect **yes**. These pioneering observations, experiments and hypotheses on psychological reversal and energy disruption are major contributions to the fields of psychotherapy and have inspired further exploration of the importance of the polarity phenomena when dealing with psychological problems.

The Energetic Influence of Beliefs

A belief is something you think is true and upon which you base your thoughts about yourself and the world in which you live. Chiropractor

James Durlacher and psychologist Fred Gallo were among the first to explore the energetic role of negative beliefs when they noticed how these beliefs interfered with and seemed to block energy psychology treatments. In addition, there are several energy psychology techniques such as Seemorg Matrix Work, Tapas Acupressure Techniques, Be Set Free Fast, and Healing from the Body Level Up that are all designed to target and release negative beliefs.

Beliefs typically start with the words, "I" or "I am." We consider them to be positive beliefs if they help you to function well in the world, allowing you to consider options and choices while connecting you to your inner strength and resilience. "I am smart, competent, or lovable" are all examples of positive beliefs.

Negative beliefs are those that limit your ability to function and attain your stated intention. They can be narrow and affect only certain areas of your life (for example, "I am a poor reader") or they can be pervasive and compromise many areas of your life (for example, "I don't deserve love and happiness").

We wish to discuss a type of negative belief, called a blocking belief. For the purposes of TAB, blocking beliefs are beliefs that compromise your mind-body-energy system. Some blocking beliefs may be painfully obvious to you while other blocking beliefs may be below your level of awareness and you will need to use the self-testing methods in Chapter 6 to uncover them. Similar to negative beliefs, they can be as simple as a belief that blocks the particular intention or goal you are trying to reach, or a pervasive negative life theme. Regardless of the severity, any blocking belief is limiting as it narrows your ability to make healthy choices in the present. They make you too afraid to try a new relationship, or contribute to your inability to speak up at work, or take care of your health. Releasing blocking beliefs will allow you to consider all of your options.

Any time you use TAB and you are unsuccessful, or you are stuck at a certain SUD or SUE level, you have discovered the source of why change is so difficult for you. You have a blocking belief that interferes with the energy of your stated intention and disorganizes your energies.

Most blocking beliefs were learned at a young age from early family experience and you can even self-test to determine how old you were when a belief started.

Frank's Predicament

Frank is a 45-year-old postal worker whose mother died after a long illness when he was four years old. He couldn't remember much about her actual death, and all he knew was that one day he and his father left their house and went to live with his father's parents. They took nothing of his mother's with them, not even a picture of her and throughout his childhood no one mentioned her name.

Frank excelled in sports, and in school and always tried to look happy, but deep inside he felt dead. He reported, "No one talked about my mom. I know they didn't know what to do with me, and maybe I didn't want them to bring it up either, but the sadness would come up every time I sat still or tried to go to sleep. All my life I have been depressed and sad."

Frank began by rubbing the NLR spot affirming, "I accept myself even though I have this sadness and grief that won't go away." He then used TAB at the side of the hand while stating his intention, "I am ready to release my sadness and grief, its roots and origins, and all that it means and does to me." He did a round of TAB on the meridians, an integration sequence and then TAB on the meridians. His SUD went down to a three, so he did another round, using the word **'completely'** *in his affirmation and intention. He again used TAB on the meridians, then an integration sequence and TAB on the meridians. This time, however, his SUD did not lower. As he focused on his body and emotions, he noticed a reluctance to release the sadness. He tried to find out what was disturbing him. A belief popped in and he amazed himself as he said, "I guess there's a part of me who connects the aching sadness to my mom. I think that if I let go of the ache, I'd let go of everything I remember about her." I am keeping connected to my mom by being sad was the belief that was blocking Frank. He self-tested, and found that this belief tested positive.*

Although Frank was disturbed when he realized this belief, he had to admit it made great sense from a child's point of view. He said, "As a child it was the

145

only option I had to connect to my mother, but now I know I can find something else that could work better. I could find someone to talk to about her, someone who knew her and I could maybe remember how it must have been maybe when I was first born, anything that could be better." He then rubbed his NLR spot and made the affirmation, "I accept myself even though a part of me is feeling disloyal to release this sadness." He reported that it felt great just to admit and honor that part of himself. He was then ready to totally release his sadness. He did another round of the TAB treatment, and his SUD level went to zero. He then visualized a heart connection to his mother. He reported feeling a very strong sense of connection to his mother throughout his entire body, and was able to experience a deep sense of peace that he had never felt before. His new belief was, "I am always connected to my mom in my heart." (You will learn the same imagining exercise that Frank used in Chapter 11.)

As you can see, because no one in Frank's family would talk about his mother, he could only remain connected to her through his sadness. His belief, "I can only stay connected to my mother by being sad" was his reality, and he held an unconscious fear that if he released his sadness he would lose all connection to her. Once Frank released his blocking belief, he was able to see that there were many other possible options to connect to his mother.

Monica's Story

Monica is a bright attractive medical secretary in her mid-30s. Whenever she has a cold or a problem, she immediately thinks that there is something terribly wrong with her. She goes on the Internet and looks up all of her symptoms, imagining the worst possible scenario. She states, "I take it to the worst possible conclusion. My family thinks I am a hypochondriac, and they are sick of listening to me."

*When Monica thought about her problem, her SUD was an eight, her stomach was tense, and her throat had a lump in it. However, her self-test was **yes** when she thought about her problem of thinking there was something wrong. She tested **no** on the statement, "I want to be over this fear of something being wrong with me (its roots, causes, and all that it means and does to me)." When she self-tested the blocking beliefs below, she was surprised to test **yes** on, "I will lose myself if I give* *up this problem." Further self-testing also revealed that the belief started before she was five. She laughed, for now it made sense to her! Her parents were constantly fighting and eventually divorced when she was four. "I constantly thought there was something wrong with me since they wouldn't stay together for me. I felt invisible to them and I had all sorts of stomachaches and problems."*

Once Monica identified the blocking belief, she used the treatment below to release the blocking belief and then work on her intention, "I want to be over this fear of something being wrong with me (its roots, causes, and all that it means and does to me)."

Identifying Blocking Beliefs in TAB

You are likely to encounter blocking beliefs at three different points during your work using TAB.

Blocking Beliefs at the Beginning of TAB Treatment

You will know a blocking belief is present at the start of the treatment because, like Monica above, your self-test will be positive (**yes**) when you think of your problem. As we have already stated, this is the opposite of what we would expect, as the negative emotion associated with a problem should cause your self-test to be negative. In addition, if you have a blocking belief, when you self-test on the statement, "I am choosing to be over this problem," your self-test will be negative (**no**).

Blocking Beliefs at the Middle or End of TAB Treatment

You will know a blocking belief is present at the middle or toward the end of treatment because you will find that after rounds of TAB treatment, your SUD or SUE level remains the same. For example, you may start at a SUD level of ten, and after two rounds of TAB the SUD level is five both times. When this happens, you should self-test using statements such as, "I am choosing to be *completely* over this problem." At this point, you may get a negative response, which will alert you that a blocking belief has been uncovered.

As we described earlier, you can try using affirmations with the word **completely** in them such as, "*I accept myself even though I do not* *want to be **completely** over this problem/fear/belief"* and intentions such as, *"I am ready to **completely** release this fear/belief/problem."* However if you continue to test **no**, then you will need to review the list of blocking beliefs below and self-test to uncover the specific belief that is blocking your progress.

The Primary Blocking Beliefs

The four primary blocking beliefs that we have found to disrupt TAB treatments usually involve issues of safety, deservedness, relationships, and the future. When evaluating which one of these blocking beliefs is currently active, it is best to use your self-knowledge and intuition to guide you where to begin. For instance, if you are working on an issue involving fear, it would be wise to evaluate the future and safety aspects early in your work. When self-esteem issues are being addressed, it would be wise to evaluate the possibility of a deservedness-related blocking belief. If you are someone who often worries about the opinions of others, then target the relationship beliefs. Often your own immediate thoughts will guide you to the correct choice. For example, if you find yourself thinking, *"I don't think I will ever be able to get over this problem,"* you may want to check yourself for a future belief-related block.

Safety Blocking Beliefs

Inherent in the *safety* blocking belief are the issues of vulnerability, risk, trust and safety, not only for oneself, but also sometimes for other loved ones. For example, if you are working on a fear of flying, you may want to check on the blocking belief around the safety, not only for self but also for others. Parents are frequently concerned about what will happen to their children should they die in a plane crash. These are healthy concerns, but the problem arises when you want to be able to fly comfortably and are phobic, or anxious about flying. While the safety blocking belief can be evident in the treatment of phobias and trauma-related experiences, it can come up in other cases. It is usually helpful to check for it with the simple question, *"What am I afraid of?"*

Deservedness Blocking Beliefs

The *deservedness* blocking belief often appears if you have negative beliefs involving shame, unworthiness, or self-condemnation. It is especially prevalent in children of alcoholics and victims of abuse. It is usually helpful to check with a question like, *"Do I think I deserve to have this problem because I am bad?"*

Future Blocking Beliefs

The *future* blocking belief carries with it the idea that you don't believe that you will ever get over the targeted problem. Often when people have a long-standing issue that they have tried many times to get over, they can be somewhat discouraged and believe they will have this particular problem forever. In these cases, it may be helpful to check for it with the question, *"What do I think will happen in the future if I am over this problem?"* or, *"Do I even think it is possible to get over this problem?"*

Relationship Blocking Beliefs

There is another common group of blocking beliefs that center around the impact of change on your *relationships*. These beliefs consider how others perceive you, and how the balance of power might be affected if you change. The major concern is frequently that if you change, you will lose the connection to the important people in your life. Sometimes even if a loved one is dead, you may fear you will lose the connection to their memory (see Frank's story). The defining question might be something like, *"What might happen to the relationship between (name of person) _____ and me if I change or release this problem/feeling/belief?"*

Another area of *relationship* beliefs centers around the impact change will have on the relationship you will have with yourself. Questions to uncover this could include, *"What will I expect of myself if I change this problem/fear/belief?"* or, *"Who will I be if I change?"* or, *"What role will I have to give up?"*

Unknown Blocking Beliefs

There will be times when you just cannot figure out what is blocking you, and yet your self-test stays **yes** when you think about your problem despite a high SUD or SUE level. Treating unknown blocking beliefs allows you the freedom to connect in with whatever it may be that is interfering with successful completion of your treatment without the words to describe the block. Remember, this is energy work and although it can be helpful to put the problem into words, it is not always necessary. Treatment of "unknown blocking beliefs" cuts through the trial-and-error process and is often the quickest way to get to a deep level of interference.

Self-Test for Blocking Beliefs

At the start of treatment, as already mentioned, there is a blocking belief if:

- You think of your problem and test **yes.**

- You state, *"I am ready/choosing to be over this problem (its roots, causes, and all that it means and does to me)"* and you test **no.**

In the middle or end of a TAB treatment, there is a blocking belief if:

- Your SUD or SUE level stays at the same level.

- You state, *"I am ready/choosing to be completely over this problem (its roots, causes, and all that it means and does to me)"* and you test **no.**

Think about Possible Blocking Beliefs

Think about your life in relation to the problem. Is there a negative life theme? Is there a rule that limits your choices? Is there a belief that may involve safety, deservedness, relationships or the future? Look at the other types of belief we have given you. Do any of them resonate?

You are not limited to one test so, if you wish, you can test as many negative beliefs as you choose, and you also may test any belief that comes to your awareness that is not listed below. In addition, you might just want to test to see if it is an unknown blocking belief that is below your level of awareness. Once you have figured out your blocking belief, move to the next section for treatment strategies.

Self-Test to Determine Blocking Beliefs

In order to determine what is blocking your progress in TAB, think about your problem, belief, or fear and self-test. Although we have given you the beliefs in categories, the categories are fluid so think of them only as guidelines. When you self-test, if you get **yes** for a belief that would compromise your goals, you should treat that belief so that you have your energetic options opened for choice.

Statements for Self-Test

The following are tables of possible statements in relation to blocking beliefs. While thinking about your problem, go down the list and self-test to the statements. You should get a **no** to the first column and a **yes** to the second. There is a blocking belief if you get **yes** on the first column. If you cannot decide whether you are getting the correct response it is suggested that you choose to treat it as a blocking belief. In other words, if in doubt, treat it.

Notice that each statement can be said with or without the words in parentheses as these words address the possible roots and causes of the problem and the potential for the problem to affect others, which usually include loved ones. When you make an affirmation or intention you may say all of the statement or only part. Your intuition will frequently play a role in choosing what you do.

Safety Blocking Beliefs

I am not safe if I release this problem/belief/fear (its roots, causes, and all that it means and does to me or others.)	Vs.	I am safe if I release this problem/belief/fear (its roots, causes, and all that it means and does to me or others.)
I am afraid my life will be out of control if I release this problem/belief/fear (its roots, causes, and all that it means and does to me or others.)	Vs.	I will be okay if I release this problem/belief/fear (its roots, causes, and all that it means and does to me or others.)
I am afraid I cannot handle options if I release this problem/belief/fear (its roots, causes, and all that it means and does to me or others.)	Vs.	I am able to handle options if I release this problem/belief/fear (its roots, causes, and all that it means and does to me or others.)
I am powerless to release this problem/belief/fear (its roots, causes, and all that it means and does to me or others.)	Vs.	I have the power to release this problem (its roots, causes, and all that it means and does to me or others.)

Deservedness Blocking Beliefs

I do not deserve to release this problem/belief/fear (its roots, causes, and all that it means and does to me or others.)	Vs.	I deserve to release this problem/belief/fear (its roots, causes, and all that it means and does to me or others.)
I am not worthy of releasing this problem/belief/fear (its roots, causes, and all that it means and does to me or others.)	Vs.	I am worthy of releasing this problem/belief/fear (its roots, causes, and all that it means and does to me or others.)

Future Blocking Beliefs

I will not release this problem/belief/fear (its roots, causes, and all that it means and does to me or others.)	Vs.	I will release this problem/belief/fear (its roots, causes, and all that it means and does to me or others.)
I will not be able to release this problem/belief/fear (its roots, causes, and all that it means and does to me or others.)	Vs.	I will be able to release this problem/belief/fear (its roots, causes, and all that it means and does to me or others.)
It will not be possible to release this problem/belief/fear (its roots, causes, and all that it means and does to me or others.)	Vs.	It will be possible to release this problem/belief/fear (its roots, causes, and all that it means and does to me or others.)

Relationship to Others Blocking Beliefs

I am afraid of being alone if I release this problem/belief/fear (its roots, causes, and all that it means and does to me or others.)	Vs.	I am okay if I release this problem/belief/fear (its roots, causes, and all that it means and does to me or others.)
I am afraid of who I will become to others if I release this problem/belief/fear (its roots, causes, and all that it means and does to me or others.)	Vs.	I am okay with who I am to others if I release this problem/belief/fear (its roots, causes, and all that it means and does to me or others.)
I am afraid my family will be upset or unhappy if I release this problem/belief/fear (its roots, causes, and all that it means and does to me or others.)	Vs.	I am okay if my family is unhappy/upset if I release this problem/belief/fear (its roots, causes, and all that it means and does to me or others.)
I am being disloyal to my family if I release this problem/belief/fear (its roots, causes, and all that it means and does to me or others.)	Vs.	I am loyal to myself if I release this problem/belief/fear (its roots, causes, and all that it means and does to me or others.)

I will lose my connection to a loved one if I release this problem/belief/fear (its roots, causes, and all that it means and does to me or others.)	Vs.	I will still be connected to my loved ones if I release this problem/belief/fear (its roots, causes, and all that it means and does to me or others.)
I won't fit in if I release this problem/belief/fear (its roots, causes, and all that it means and does to me or others.)	Vs.	I am okay if I release this problem/belief/ fear (its roots, causes, and all that it means and does to me or others.)

Relationship to Self Blocking Beliefs

I will loose my identity if I release this problem/belief/fear (its roots, causes, and all that it means and does to me or others.)	Vs.	I will keep my real identity if I release this problem/belief/fear (its roots, causes, and all that it means and does to me or others.)
I can't trust myself if I release this problem/belief/fear (its roots, causes, and all that it means and does to me or others.)	Vs.	I can trust myself if I release this problem/belief/fear (its roots, causes, and all that it means and does to me or others.)
I can't handle making decisions myself if I release this problem/belief/fear (its roots, causes, and all that it means and does to me or others.)	Vs.	I can handle making decisions myself if I release this problem/belief/fear(its roots, causes, and all that it means and does to me or others.)
I lack the willpower to release this problem/belief/fear (its roots, causes, and all that it means and does to me or others.)	Vs.	I have the willpower to release this problem/belief/fear (its roots, causes, and all that it means and does to me or others.)
I will be deprived if I release this problem/belief/fear (its roots, causes, and all that it means and does to me or others.)	Vs.	I will be okay if I release this problem/belief/fear (its roots, causes, and all that it means and does to me or others.)

I am too stupid to release this problem/belief/fear (its roots, causes, and all that it means and does to me or others.)	Vs.	I am smart enough to release this problem/belief/fear (its roots, causes, and all that it means and does to me or others.)
I am powerless to release this problem/belief/fear (its roots, causes and all that it means and does to me or others.)	Vs.	I have the power to release this problem (its roots, causes, and all that it means and does to me or others)

Unknown Blocking Belief

There is an unknown belief blocking my releasing this problem/belief/fear (its roots, causes, and all that it means and does to me and others.)	Vs.	There is no unknown belief blocking my releasing this problem/belief/fear (its roots, causes, and all that it means and does to me and others.)

When Blocks Occur Toward the End of Treatment

As mentioned previously, blocks can occur at any point in the treatment, but frequently we have seen a client's polarity disorganize and block the treatment as the problem was getting close to being eliminated (SUD or SUE level four or lower). In the same way that you use *completely* during the steps you learned in Chapter 4, you can use the word *completely* when dealing with a specific blocking belief. For example, if your blocking belief is, *"I am unsafe to be free of this problem"* and TAB lowers the SUD, but not to zero, then self-test on, *"I am safe if I am **completely** free of this problem (its roots, causes, and all that it means and does to me and others)"* vs. *"I am not safe if I am **completely** free of this problem (its roots, causes and all that it means and does to me and others)."*

Treatment for Beliefs that Block Intentions and Goals

In treating blocking beliefs we always use both affirmations and statements of intention. As noted in Chapter 3, affirmations are statements that accept the position you are in currently. For example, *"I accept myself even though I believe I don't deserve a healthy relationship."* On the other hand, statements of intention focus on a direction and goal you wish to take and your primary concerns are toward the future. Once you have discovered the belief that is blocking your progress, you will rub the NLR spot making an affirmation that accepts where the belief is right now. We have found it is important to make this affirmation with compassion for yourself.

If you have difficulty making an affirmation with an empathetic stance, you can treat this as a problem in the same way that you treat any other blocking belief. For example, while rubbing the NLR, you could make the statement, *"I accept myself even though I do not believe I can accept myself."*

You will then TAB at the side of your hand with a statement of intention to release this belief. *"I am choosing to release my belief that I cannot accept myself."* This could also be phrased as, *"I am choosing to release my belief that I have to be so hard on myself, its roots, causes, and all that it means and does to me and to others."*

Steps to Release a Blocking Belief

We will now go through an example of how to use these techniques on a common blocking belief: *"I am unsafe and others are unsafe if I am over this problem, (its roots, causes, and all that it means and does to me and to others.)"*

Correction at NLR with an Affirmation

Rub the NLR and say three times: *"I accept myself even though I have this belief that I am unsafe and others are unsafe if I am over this problem (its roots, causes, and all that it means and does to me and to others)."*

(Picture 8.1)

Picture 8.1
Rubbing the NLR

Correction at Side of Hand with an Intention

While holding the side of your hand say three times, *"I am choosing/ready to release the blocking belief that I am unsafe and others are unsafe if I let go of this problem, (its roots, causes, and all that it means and does to me)."* (Picture 8.2)

Picture 8.2
Mindfully Stating Intention

Check the Correction

It is especially important, once you have made a correction using affirmations and intentions, that you check your correction with a self-test. If the correction worked, you will expect a **yes** self-test to the healthier belief, and a **no** self-test to the original blocking belief.

For example, a **yes** self-test should result when you say, *"I am safe and others are safe if I am over this problem."* And a **no** self-test should occur when saying, *"I am unsafe or others are unsafe if I am over this problem."* If the correction above does not work for you, you will need to treat the blocking belief as its own problem using the information in the next chapter as your guide.

James Revisited

*James, the 29-year-old dad described earlier in the chapter, decided he wanted to release the rest of his anger about his ex-wife. Although he tested **no** at the mere mention of her name (**no** is the correct direction because her name is a problem), he also tested **no** at the stated intention, "I am choosing to release my anger." (James should test **yes** with this intention.) It was clear that his energies were disrupted on the intention to release his anger, which signified a blocking belief. He wasn't surprised; he said that he felt entitled to his anger, and was able to admit to himself that actually he felt good being angry. "It beats feeling vulnerable and depressed!" Noticing some level of pleasure in this, he rated the enjoyment he experiences with his anger at a five on the SUE scale.*

He self-tested several blocking beliefs, and realized he had a positive self-test to the belief, "I am unsafe if I release this." He thought about it, and decided that maybe he would have been unsafe to release his anger a year ago, but there was no danger now, as he was really happier being out of the marriage. He said the divorce was actually the best thing that had happened to him and that, if he were truly honest with himself, he should actually be thanking the guy with whom she had the affair. Although he never wanted to get a divorce for his children's sake, he also had to admit that they were thriving without the constant tension in the house that had been there prior to the affair. He thought about his current anger and the impact on his children and then he made an affirmation, "I accept myself even though I am enjoying being angry," and rubbed the NLR spot. He then used

TAB at the side of the hand, and restated his intention, "I am choosing to release my anger now." Using the full TAB treatment he was able to release the rest of the anger, and his SUD and SUE were both at a zero. After treatment, self-testing revealed, he could stay strong at the mention of her name. He was now able to be cordial and respectful of her for the sake of his children.

Moving on to Chapter Nine

You have now learned ways to correct your mind-body-energy when it is impacted by negative thoughts and blocking beliefs. You will find these tools especially valuable when you have a belief that contradicts your stated intention and goal. Now you are ready for the next chapter where you will learn how to take any belief that negatively influences you, and shift it to a healthier belief.

CHAPTER 9

The Energetic Impact of Core Beliefs

In this chapter we continue to discuss the negative impact of beliefs on your mind-body-energy system and we make an arbitrary but useful distinction between beliefs that block your stated intention, and beliefs that are more pervasive in your life, requiring a deeper level of treatment. We will teach you strategies to determine these beliefs and how to use TAB to shift the energy of any negative belief to provide the energy for a healthier one. As in other chapters, we use case examples to help you to pinpoint what might be the belief behind your distress.

Core Beliefs

In our clinical practices there are sometimes patients for whom the simple corrections of rubbing the NLR with an affirmation and TAB at the side-of-hand with an intention weren't fully effective in shifting a strongly held core belief. In these cases, we found that you could efficiently treat the belief with TAB using the same steps as you used for any other problem. In this chapter you will learn how to treat a core belief of any kind.

Generational Core Beliefs

Beliefs can be passed down through generations. For example, some families have passed along the belief, *"Don't trust anyone but family."* Other beliefs might be, *"I am poor, and there is never enough money."* It is understandable why a person would test **no** when saying, *"I want to release this belief,"* because it is a belief that a part of them may think is protecting and keeping them safe. Other times beliefs seem to be the "rules of life" or the way things are "supposed to be" and you go on believing them as if they were fact, as it might seem disloyal to do anything different.

Carol's Story

Carol is a 49-year-old psychological therapist who specializes in addiction therapy. As a young child her father was an alcoholic who was frequently out of work. The family moved on many occasions, and sometimes with just a day's notice. Nothing ever felt safe and secure. She began to feel powerful when, at age twelve, she got a job, and earned her own money. Now, in her own successful private practice, she has plenty of money, but she is still extremely afraid of being poor again. This impacts every area of her life. She says, "I hide my money; I work long hours for extra money; I put up with my mean live-in because I am afraid of the expenses if I live alone. I am afraid all the time." When asked what she would do if given a million dollars, she knew exactly the changes she would make in her life; but without the actual cash in hand, she felt stuck.

Carol's beliefs included:

- *I am not safe without money*
- *I will be a bag lady without money*
- *I will be humiliated without money*
- *I am less than others*
- *I never have enough*

Tenacious Core Beliefs

Some beliefs are tenacious. In childhood, if your parent is traumatized by a life event and does not get help, you may develop beliefs about yourself and the world to make sense of how you are treated. It is not unusual for people to comment that someone is "just not the same" since they came back from the war, or since their child died. On some level, you can appreciate the enormity of these life events, but because of the loss the tragedy continues for others in the family when the victims can't forgive themselves, or can't get the trauma images out of their minds.

Jackson's Story

Jackson's father was traumatized by his war experiences and carried the trauma to his family. Jackson developed the core belief while growing up under emotionally debilitating circumstances that, "If something good happens, then something bad will follow," or, "I will pay a price for having fun."

Jackson's father was a Vietnam veteran and as is the case so often with vets, his father witnessed many friends being killed in ambushes and horrific battles. When he returned from the war, his father married and he and his wife had six children. He could never handle noise and chaos at home, as it unconsciously reminded him of war. Whenever, Jackson and his siblings were excited and playful, their father would respond with agitation and violence. Inevitably, someone always got hit, at times violently. Jackson's mom always tried to keep the children quiet and the house clean so his father did not get upset. No one understood the concept of emotional triggers, or how the commotion and chaos could trigger agitation and anger in Jackson's father because he was being unconsciously reminded of the time he lost his friends in battle. Jackson and his siblings grew up believing that there was something wrong with being excited and playful and that something bad would happen if they were having fun.

Jackson is now married with three small children, and he experiences his own intense agitation and fear when they are noisy and having fun. "It feels like something is wrong, and I have to silence them." For Jackson, noise is a trigger to his own frightening childhood and whenever he starts to relax and have fun, he fears something bad will happen to him (as it had when he was a young boy.) He also finds this belief surfaces when he is at the office, or relaxing with co-workers. Using self-testing, Jackson was able to identity that he had the belief: "If I am having fun something bad will happen."

Compare Jackson's story to Peter's situation and notice how important and helpful it is to family and loved ones to treat the victim of a traumatic event.

Peter's Story

Peter is a 52-year-old successful banker whose son, John, had been killed in a car accident two years before. John had a long history of gambling, and the accident occurred immediately after he'd had a phone conversation with his father in which Peter had angrily refused to bail John out of his current gambling debts. For the past two years the only memories Peter had of his son was arriving on the accident scene and seeing the blood. Peter was devastated and guilty, blaming himself for the accident. "I can't feel happiness now; I should have given him the money. My own life ended that day too." He reports he can no longer feel any joy and his wife and children say he just sits and stares; even his new grandchildren mean nothing to him.

The major difference between Jackson's father and Peter is that Peter finally agreed to seek psychotherapy. Peter was able to use TAB to release the traumatic images, bringing about a shift in his beliefs that allowed him to participate in life once again. We discuss Peter's treatment later in the chapter.

Identifying Pervasive Core Beliefs

The following are ways to determine what your core beliefs might be. Consider core beliefs as "life themes" that usually impact your world in numerous ways. It is often helpful to write a paragraph about your current life situation, or talk about it with a trusted friend, listening especially for any **I** or **I am** negative statements.

It can also be helpful to write down the words **I am** and then quickly follow it with ten statements, noticing which ones are negative and can be the focus of your self-treatment.

Sample:

I am _____ *(undeserving, always getting hurt...)*

I am _____

*I am*_____

Because beliefs can be below your level of awareness, it is some-time helpful to self-test further to get additional clarity on the impact of a belief, such as where and how it started. You can even self-test to determine what percentage of you believes a certain belief.

Sample self-testing questions:

I have had this belief since I was:

Under the age of 5 _____

Under the age of 10 _____

Under the age of 15, etc. _____

You can also self-test for a specific age _____

All of me believes _____

Part of me (i.e., 50%) believes _____

This is a family belief _____

Number of generations _____

The Language You Heard Growing Up

If you grew up speaking a language other than English, write these thoughts in your native language so you can access the part of your mind that holds the core belief. Also, say your affirmations and intentions in your native language for the same reason.

Treatment of Core Beliefs

Once you have identified the negative core belief that you wish to change, the next step is to choose the belief that you would like to have in its place. As a way to measure your progress, you will make an adjustment to the rating scales we have already given you. Think of your replacement belief, and rate how true it feels to you on a zero to ten scale, where zero is not true at all and ten is completely true. For example, if your negative belief is, "I am stupid" and you want to believe "I am smart enough," think to yourself "I am smart enough," and rate how true it feels at this point. There is no right or wrong belief. You only need to choose a belief that allows you to have more options to live a happier and healthier life.

Another important concept in shifting the energy in core beliefs is to make sure that you say your accepting affirmation in a sincere way. While this is important throughout TAB, we have seen patients become frustrated and unloving toward themselves as these old, unhelpful beliefs surface. Please be especially aware of that tendency here. Remember that this core belief is likely one that you have had since childhood, and that these types of beliefs make sense to children, as it is how they make sense of difficult and often painful situations. Have compassion for yourself. Be thankful that you are releasing negative beliefs now. Remember that a key concept of mindfulness is to examine your thoughts without judgment! If you have a difficult time making affirmations to accept yourself, and have tried the techniques in Chapter 8, you may want to use the treatment below to work on the belief, "*I am not allowed to be compassionate toward myself.*"

Finally, it is usually important to add the following statement to affirmations and intentions: "*its roots, causes, and all that it means and does to me and to others*" (Diepold, Britt & Bender, 2004). While you may not always need this statement in TAB, we find it to be especially helpful when working with core beliefs, as it instructs the system to go to the core of the problem and the impact of the belief on your current life functioning.

Steps to Treat Core Beliefs

Start by getting comfortable, drink some water, and massage your neck and shoulders. Think about your belief and notice the area/s of your body that is/are involved. Get a SUD & SUE level, make an affirmation, state an intention, treat the fourteen points, do the integration sequence, then treat the fourteen points again. End with an eye-roll.

Step 1: Identify the Belief That You Would Like to Change

Identify the negative core belief that you would like to change, and choose a positive belief that you would like to substitute.

Write down your negative belief: _____

_____

Write down your positive belief: _____

_____

As a way to measure your progress, remember you will make an adjustment to the rating scales we have already given you. As you think of your positive belief, please rate how true it feels to you on a zero to ten scale, where zero is not true at all and ten is completely true.

Write down how true it feels at the beginning of your work:_____

_____

Step 2: Notice any Signs of Distress in Your Body

Focus your mind on the amount of distress the negative belief causes you in the present moment, by scanning for any tension or disturbance in your body. If your belief has an element of enjoyment, focus your mind on the enjoyment and notice any areas of your body where you feel the enjoyment.

My body sensations are _____

_____

Step 3: Rate Your Distress with SUD and SUE Levels

SUD

Rate the amount of distress you are experiencing on a scale from zero to ten where zero is no distress and ten is the worst you could experience. (Use the SUD scale in Chapter 2.)

My SUD level is _____

SUE

Rate the amount of enjoyment you are experiencing, even though you know this belief is not good for you, or causes grief for those you love, on a scale from zero to ten where zero is no enjoyment and ten is the most enjoyment you could experience. (Use the SUE scale in Chapter 2.) Remember what is important for SUE is the amount of enjoyment, even though it is not good for you.

My SUE level is _____

If you have both SUD and SUE levels, work on the distress (SUD) first. When your SUD is low, then work on the enjoyment (SUE).

Step 4: Rub the NLR and Make an Affirmation

Cross your hands over your chest, and rub with deep pressure the area beneath your hands. You may find the spots are a bit sorem which is normal.

State an affirmation three times. (Picture 9.1)

Picture 9.1
Rubbing NLR

I accept myself even though I believe (state the belief here) _____

_____

(its roots, causes, and all that it means and does to me and those I love.)

Step 5: State an Intention at the Side of Your Hand

State an intention for change as you touch the side of your hand and take a deep breath through your nose. (Picture 9.2)

Picture 9.2

Mindfully State Your Intention

While touching the side-of-hand meridian spot, state an intention, such as *"I am ready/choosing to release my belief* (state the belief) _____ _____ *(its*

roots, causes, and all that it means and does to me and those I love.)"

Do this three times.

Step 6: Mindfully Touch-and-Breathe on Each of the Fourteen Meridian Points

Think about your negative belief. Touch each meridian treatment point and take a deep breath in and out at each point. You may take as many breaths as you like before moving on to the next point. (Use Illustration 9.1 as your guide.)

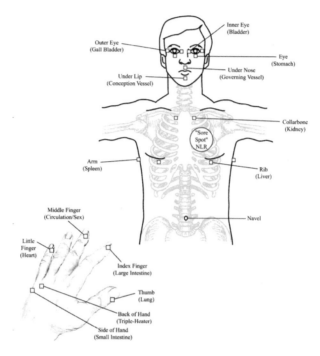

Illustration 9.1
TAB Treatment Point Locations

The basic sequence is as follows:

1. Inner Eye

2. Outer Eye

3. Under Eye

4. Under Nose

5. Under Lip

6. Under Arm

7. Rib/Under Breast

8. Thumb

9. Index Finger

10. Middle Finger

11. Little Finger

12. Back of hand

13. Side of hand

14. Collarbone

Step 7: Do the Brain Integration

Touch both collarbone treatment points at the same time using the tip of your thumb on one point and tips of your index, middle and ring fingers on the other point. *With your other hand, use your index, middle and ring fingers to touch the back of hand treatment spot of the hand on your collarbone points.* (See Picture 9.3)

Picture 9.3
Hand Position for Integration Sequence

1. Close eyes

2. Open eyes

3. Eyes look down to right

4. Eyes look down to left

5. Rotate the eyes in one full circle

6. Rotate the eyes in one full circle in the other direction

7. Hum a tune (for approximately five to seven seconds)

8. Count from one to five

9. Hum a tune again (for approximately five to seven seconds)

Step 8: Repeat the Treatment Sequence

Touch each of the fourteen meridian treatment points again, taking as many breaths at each point as you feel you need.

Step 9: Check Your Work-Rate — Your SUD and SUE Levels

Focus on your belief again.

Rate your distress on a scale from zero to ten. Did it get better, worse or stay the same? Rate your SUE in the same way.

My SUD is _____ *My SUE is* _____

If your SUD and SUE are two or lower, go to Step 16, the eye-roll procedure. If your SUD and SUE are more than two, go to Step 10.

Step 10: Make an Affirmation Accepting that Your Self-Work is Incomplete

Rub the NLR spot as you state an affirmation. (See Picture 9.1)

Affirmation formula: *I accept myself even though I am not completely over this belief (state the belief)* _____ *(its roots, causes, and all that it means and does to me and those I love).*

I accept myself even though I still believe some of this negative belief (state the belief) _____ *(its roots, causes, and all that it means and does to me and those I love).*

Step 11: State an Intention for "Complete" Change

State an intention to *completely* release the belief as you touch the side of your hand. (See Picture 9.2)

I am ready/choosing to completely release this belief _____ _____ *(its roots, causes, and all that it means and does to me and those I love).*

Step 12: Mindfully Touch and Breathe on Each of the Fourteen Points

Step 13: Do the Brain Integration Sequence

Step 14: Repeat the Treatment Sequence

Mindfully Touch and Breathe on each of the fourteen points

Step 15: Check Your SUD and SUE Levels

If SUD and SUE are two or less, go to Step 16. If more than two, go back to Step 10 and repeat Steps 10 to 15. When your SUD and SUE become two or less, go on to Step 16. If you have gone through this more than three times, you will need to check for a blocking belief (Chapter 8), and treat that belief first; (i.e., *it is not safe to let go of this negative belief*).

Step 16: End of Treatment Eye-Roll

Touch both collarbone treatment points at the same time using the tip of your thumb on one point and tips of your index, middle and ring fingers on the other point. With your other hand, use your index, middle and ring fingers to touch the back of hand treatment spot of the hand on your collarbone points. (See Picture 9.4)

Picture 9.4
Hand Position for Eye-Roll

While holding the points, take one full respiration, drawing your mind energy to the points. Maintain contact with the collarbone points. Close your eyes. Open your eyes. Looking straight ahead, drop your eyes to the ground and slowly roll your eyes up to the sky taking five to seven seconds from ground to sky. At the top, relax back to a comfortable position.

Step 17: Focus on Your New Positive Belief

Focus on your positive belief

Rate how true the belief feels now

Rate 0–10 _____(ten means it feels completely true)

If your belief is eight or higher, go to Step 25 and do the eye-roll. If your belief is eight or less, go to Step 18.

Step 18: Make an Affirmation

Rub the NLR spot (see Picture 9.1) and state your affirmation.

I accept myself even though I do not completely believe this new belief (state the belief) _____.

Make this affirmation three times.

Step 19: State Your Intention

While using TAB at the side-of-hand (see Picture 9.2), state your intention:

I am ready/choosing to completely believe this new belief (state the belief)
_____.

State this intention three times.

Step 20: Mindfully Touch and Breathe on Each of the Fourteen Points

Step 21: Do the Brain Integration Sequence

Step 22: Repeat the Treatment Sequence

Mindfully Touch and Breathe on each of the fourteen points.

Step 23: Focus on Your New Positive Belief

Focus on your positive belief

Rate how true the belief feels now

Rate 0–10 _____(ten means it feels completely true)

If your belief is 8 or higher, go to Step 25, the eye-roll. If your belief is eight or less, but is feeling stronger, repeat Steps 18 through 24. It may take several rounds to get it to an eight or better. If it doesn't go to an eight after several rounds, go back to Chapter 8 and check for unknown or other possible blocking beliefs.

Step 24: End of Treatment Eye-Roll

Touch both collarbone treatment points at the same time using the tip of your thumb on one point and tips of your index, middle and ring fingers on the other point. With your other hand, use your index, middle and ring fingers to touch the back of hand treatment spot of the hand on your collarbone points. (See Picture 9.5)

Picture 9.5
Hand Position for Eye-Roll

While holding the points, take one full respiration, drawing your mind energy to the points. Maintain contact with the collarbone points. Close your eyes. Open your eyes. Looking straight ahead, drop your eyes to the ground and slowly roll your eyes up to the sky taking five to seven seconds from ground to sky. At the top, relax back to a comfortable position.

Case Examples

Below are several examples demonstrating the use of TAB for beliefs. Because some beliefs originate or are held in place by traumatic events, we are including some illustrations of trauma here. However, we want to remind you that when suffering with a diagnosable mental health condition such as depression or Post Traumatic Stress Disorder, we recommend that you use these techniques with a trained clinician. This is especially important if the traumatic memory is one in which you were physically hurt such as in a car accident, a robbery, or any type of sexual or physical abuse. As you will see in Peter's situation TAB will not remove the memory, but TAB will help to process a traumatic memory so that you do not have to continue to relive it every time you think of it.

Peter's Story Continued

Peter, whose son John was killed in the car accident, only saw a therapist at the insistence of his family. He was full of grief and guilt. "I just can't get those images of the accident out of my head. My wife makes me go to those meetings with other parents who have lost a child, and all I see is the accident. It tortures me. I can't even say his name because I feel so guilty."

Peter knew he couldn't continue like this. He agreed that he would try TAB on the images of the accident. While recognizing that this wouldn't bring his son back, he did want to be able to talk about his son again with his wife. He and his therapist used the TAB protocol on the images, having him imagine them and then make an affirmation, "I accept myself even though I didn't give John the money he wanted and this happened." This was a hard statement to say, although he knew giving John more money wouldn't have been the solution either. His intention became, "I am ready to release these horrible images."

He used TAB and, as might be suspected, a blocking belief surfaced. Because traumatic images are so strong, they block out all the good memories too. His blocking belief was, "What if I can't remember John at all? It is disloyal to do this." The therapist explained to Peter that once he removed the traumatic memories, he would be able to remember the good ones, such as John playing baseball in high school. He was relieved. He was then able to use TAB, and although it took several rounds of treatment, the vivid images of the bloody accident scene faded.

Once the traumatic images were cleared, the therapist worked with Peter on his belief that, "I don't deserve to be happy again." He felt that he wanted to replace it with, "I can be at peace for my family; John would want this." He used the TAB steps and was able to release the old belief. He was able to admit that he really was a good father, although not a perfect one, and he was able to forgive himself. He and the therapist then used an imagining technique to create a different image of his connection to John. (This imagining technique will be described in Chapter 11.)

Ruth's Story

Ruth grew up in a household where the children were always supposed to be serious and studious. "My parents came to the United States as immigrants, having both lost their families the generation before in the Holocaust. We had to achieve, study, and always be producing. As children, if we were laughing or having fun, we would be shamed and told to be quiet and to get busy doing something productive. Even when playing musical instruments we had to be constantly practicing and it was never enjoyable. I grew up believing fun was wrong and I would feel guilty automatically if something good was happening and I hadn't earned it. I always had to look busy and productive so as not to upset my parents.

At the age of 32, I was diagnosed with CFS [chronic fatigue syndrome]. My doctor told me that although the cause of chronic fatigue was unknown, one of the important parts of treatment was to become involved in an activity like meditation or yoga. I knew that I had to practice slowing down and relaxing, but each time I tried, I got nervous and anxious. I went to a meditation class and it was a dismal failure."

As Ruth sat with herself, she realized she held the belief that relaxing was bad. "I am bad if I am not being productive."

Self-testing revealed she had held the belief since she was four, and that this belief had been in her family for two generations. She wasn't surprised, because she said it felt like a form of survivor guilt. She also knew it felt disloyal to her family and ancestors to release it, and her self-test confirmed that. Therefore, there were two core beliefs that needed to be treated, "I am bad if I relax," and "I am disloyal if I release this belief." Her SUD level was a ten.

She decided she wanted her new belief to be, "I am loyal to myself and my children if I learn to relax."

She rubbed the NLR spot and accepted her present state, "I accept myself even though I believe I am bad and disloyal to my ancestors if I relax." She used TAB on the side of the hand with her intention, "I am choosing to release my belief that I am bad and disloyal to my ancestors if I relax." She used TAB on each of the meridian points, followed by the brain integration sequence, and then repeated TAB on the meridian points.

Her SUD went to a three, so she repeated the affirmation and intention with the word **completely** in the statements. Her affirmation was, "I accept myself even though I believe that I am bad and disloyal to my ancestors if I relax completely its roots, its causes, and all that it means and does to me." Her intention was, "I am choosing to completely release my belief that I am bad and disloyal to my ancestors if I relax." After doing another round of TAB on the meridians, then the brain integration sequence and TAB on the meridian points again, her SUD was a zero. She did a self-test on the new belief, "I am loyal to myself and my children if I learn to relax," and she was at a ten. She felt a wave of excitement and relaxation come over her. She ended with an eye-roll to complete her work.

Alexandra's Story

Alexandra, the Slavic language professor described in Chapter 2, (whose parents fought in Russian and finally divorced) discovered through self-testing that she had the belief, "I am not good enough" and upon reflection, realized it permeated every area of her life. She worked too long and hard in an effort to "prove herself," was uncomfortable with both male and female colleagues, and never seemed to be able to attract a healthy friendship with a man. She decided to *replace this pervasive negative belief with a new belief: "I am good enough to attract and enjoy friendships." She began with the negative belief, rubbed the NLR spot making the affirmation (in both Russian and English): "I accept myself, even though I believe I don't deserve good friends (its roots, causes, and all that it means and does to me)." She then stated an intention (in both Russian and English): "I am choosing to release the belief that I don't deserve good friends (its roots, causes, and all that it means and does to me." After reducing the SUD to a zero on the negative belief she self-tested her positive belief, "I am good enough." This tested at a seven, so she did another round of treatment in order to strengthen the positive belief. She began by rubbing the NLR saying, "I accept myself even though I do not completely believe I am good enough to deserve good friends," then used TAB at the side of the hand and stated her intention, "I am choosing to completely believe I am good enough to have good friends" and did another round of treatment. Her belief was strong now, at a ten, and she did an eye-roll treatment just to add strength to the new belief. She felt positive, strong, and worthy!*

Moving on to Chapter Ten

You have now learned ways to treat any belief that impacts your current intentions or your life in general and you will find these invaluable tools when dealing with old beliefs that began in childhood. We encourage you to follow this treatment on any belief that is no longer serving you, thus shifting the energy to a healthier belief. You are now ready to learn the focus areas associated with the treatment points learned in Chapter 4. You will also learn ways to increase your self-awareness and intuition in the next chapter.

CHAPTER 10

Personalized TAB to
Increase Intuition & Self-Awareness

Now you are ready to combine the meridian basics you learned in Chapters 4 and 5 with the self-tests you learned in Chapter 6 and integrate it all together with the new information you will learn in this chapter. We introduce you to the concept of focus areas, the areas of your body associated with the meridian treatment points. Rather than using the treatment points in generic sequence, you will use these focus areas along with your emotions and intuition to develop personalized sequences in TAB. Doing this process has the potential to increase your level of self-understanding and awareness.

You will be learning about the emotions that have been associated with each focus area and this is especially important for you if you have difficulty connecting to your feelings, or if you have a hard time identifying what you are feeling. Frequently in our clinical practice we see patients who were either directly or indirectly shamed about feeling something in response to an experience, or were told that an emotion such as anger or sadness was bad or wrong. Sometimes, a childhood experience as simple as being told to *"stop crying and acting like a baby,"* can result in difficulty connecting to feelings as an adult.

Thoughts and Emotions Influence the Meridian System

Your thoughts and emotions influence both the **physical you** and the **energy you**. As discussed earlier, Traditional Chinese Medicine does not distinguish between your mind and body, so the influence of thoughts and emotions on the meridian system must be explained in Western terms.

Focus Areas & Emotions

The meridian treatment points that you used in Chapter 4 are named for the area of the body with which the meridian is associated. You could see that the little finger treatment point is called "little finger" and heart (HT–9). This means the point you treat is on the little finger, and the heart is the organ which is associated with this meridian. You know where your heart is in your body and you also know when you are feeling an emotion that involves your heart. This connection between meridians and emotions becomes very important when treating psychological issues and you will use them as clues to determine which treatment points require your attention.

Self-testing on the different focus areas might very well lead you to some interesting discoveries about yourself! As clinicians, we have found that it is not unusual when self-testing for an emotion that is on the surface that it covers another emotion which lies beneath it. For example, a person outwardly expressing anger may test **yes** at the lung focal area. When the person connects deeply with their lung focal area, with openness to allow whatever is really bothering them to emerge, much to their amazement, they discover hidden grief, usually covered up by a blocking belief that it is not safe/right/manly to cry. We explain to people that they need not worry if something comes up. Once the grief is expressed, and TAB is used, the emotion is released and the person then experiences peace and integration.

Meridians and Associated Emotions

Remember that signals in the thought fields sometimes result in emotions that take away your behavioral choices, and bring about unwanted consequences. The exercises in the first two chapters were designed to give you awareness of your mind-body-energy connection. You noticed how a pleasant thought resonated in your body and you also experienced how an unpleasant thought resonated in your body. Together with information about the contents of thought fields, you learned to associate the pleasant resonance in your body to *elater* influence and the unpleasant resonance to *perturbation* influence. The common name given to these influences when experienced in the body is *emotion*. As you notice the part of your body that resonates or holds an emotion, you can think about that part of you in relation to a particular meridian. The meridians you are using for treatment are almost all organ related.

Negative Emotions

Since naming an emotion is so much a part of the Western culture of psychotherapy, we have decided to give you a Westerner's guide to negative emotions and meridian correlations. This is only a guide for two reasons: first, there has been no definitive proof of any one-to-one correlation of an emotion linked to a single organ or meridian. The second reason is that what you call anger may not be the same feeling in your body as the way someone else feels in their body when they use the word anger.

Remember this is only a guide for identifying negative emotions to help you begin to personalize TAB while you think about your problem.

A Handy Guide of Meridian-Negative Emotion Correlations

The meridian-emotion correlations shown in List 10.1 are from Traditional Chinese Medicine (TCM) literature (Diepold, Britt, & Bender, 2004). Note that the list is composed solely of negative emotions. As we've stressed negative emotions (*perturbations* in the thought field) are only part of the story. Positive emotions (*elaters*) are equally important.

As shown with *The Candy Cane Effect* described in Chapter 2, your self-treatment must consider the positive emotions you experience, which may be keeping negative emotions in place. For example: the good feelings you have while computer game playing keep you from experiencing the negative ones related to your work schedule.

Remember that these are only **guidelines** for using your inner resources to identify and treat the negative signals *(perturbations)* in thought fields. As you explore these connections, you may also begin to identify which meridians relate to some of your positive ones *(elaters)*.

List 10.1

The Focus Area–Treatment Point–Emotion Summary

Focus areas are usually located in the area where a particular organ is in your body. For example, the heart focus area is where the heart is located, and the gall bladder focus area is where the gall bladder is located, etc. Don't worry if you do not know exactly where an organ is; this is energy work, not surgery! You need only to think about or imagine the area of your body for your system to tell you that particular meridian needs treatment. Most of the focus areas are self-evident, and we have added pictures or a verbal description for the less obvious ones such as the governing vessel, the central vessel, circulation/sex (pericardium), and the triple heater.

- *Bladder Focus Area: Treatment Point BL-1 or Inner Eye*

  The bladder meridian is a mixture of emotions involving fear, frustration, sadness, and hypervigilance. It is associated with trauma experience, so if you suspect trauma to be part of your problem you may want to self-test the bladder focus area.

- *Gall Bladder Focus Area: Treatment Point GB-1 or Outer Eye*

  The gall bladder treatment point is associated with emotions such as rage, excess anger, fury, wrath, and powerlessness. Some patients have described rage as a combination of anger and helplessness. This point is also connected with self-loathing, when a person turns the anger on himself or herself. Sometimes it results in emotional exhaustion and poor or rash decisions.

- *Stomach Focus Area: Treatment Point ST-1 or Under Your Eye*

The stomach treatment point correlates with feelings of disgust, bitterness, fear, or anxiety. You might say you have a "knot" or "butterflies" in your stomach. In both Western and Eastern medicine, stomach ulcers have traditionally been associated with anxiety and stress.

- *Kidney Focus Area: Treatment Point K-27 or Collarbone*

The treatment point may connect to fear and fright, indecision, cowardice, lack of sexual interest, and lack of self-confidence.

- *Spleen/Pancreas Focus Area: Treatment Point SP-21 or Under Arm*

This meridian is associated with worry and anxiety for the future. It is also the treatment point for the feelings of terror that one might experience during a trauma. Not surprisingly, the spleen meridian figures in issues of your self-esteem, which we discuss in Chapter 11.

- *Liver Focus Area: Treatment Point LV-14 or Rib*

Throughout Western and Eastern cultures, the liver has been associated with anger, particularly when the anger tends to be excessive, pervasive, and is generally directed at all things, not just one specific target. The liver focus area is also the treatment point for severe impatience.

- *Large Intestine Focus Area: Treatment Point LI-1 or Index Finger*

Interestingly, the feeling most associated with the large intestines is guilt and the finger you treat it with is the index finger. Isn't that the one pointed and shaken at you when you did something wrong? It is often the meridian needed if someone is in a dysfunctional relationship or has problems with attachment like Roman, the financier, in Chapter 1.

- *Lung Focus Area: Treatment Point LU-11 or Thumb*

  The hallmark emotions for this meridian are sadness and grief. It is interesting to note that in Western tradition, lung cancer used to be called the "disease of the hopeless." For example, physicians will sometimes tell stories of older patients who have recently lost a spouse, succumbing to lung cancer within a very short time after their loved one's death. Other feelings involved with the lung meridian are prejudice, intolerance, and disdain.

- *Circulation/Sex Focus Area: Treatment Point CX-9 or Middle Finger*

  This treatment point plays a large role if you have a problem with impulse control, addictive type behavior, are extremely jealous, or stubborn. It is frequently prominent in problems that involve your sexuality and your physical health. This is interesting in view of the new information about the signaling potential of connective tissue and its location around the heart and interface with the lungs. (See Picture 10.1)

Picture 10.1
Circulation/Sex Focus Area

- *Small Intestine Focus Area: Treatment Point SI-3 or Side of Hand*

  This treatment point is also used when you state an intention. It is a particularly important when you feel vulnerable or unsafe. It is linked to unwanted thoughts, perfectionism, over-responsibility, and procrastination.

- *Heart Focus Area: Treatment Point HT-9 or Little Finger*

  This is the third meridian, whose dominant negative emotion is anger. But while the gall bladder's anger is more rageful, and the liver's anger is more pervasive, the anger of the heart meridian tends to be specifically directed at a particular person or target. It is frequently related to vengeance and control issues.

- *Triple Heater or Thyroid Focus Area (Just Below Navel) Treatment Point TH-3 or Back of Jand*

  This area is frequently needed if you are experiencing depression, sadness, and hopelessness from early childhood situations. Interestingly, it is also linked to pain management, but this may be because old childhood feelings of hopelessness may be linked in with the experience of pain you cannot control.

- *Governing Vessel Focus Area: Treatment Point GV-27 or Under Nose*

  The feelings linked with this area involve embarrassment, willpower, inferiority, and lack of power. As distinct from the gall bladder, this lack of power concerns never having had adequate power or the ability to manipulate one's environment satisfactorily. Interestingly, money and employment issues tend to be evident with this meridian.

Picture 10.2
Governing Vessel Focus Area

- *Conception Vessel Focus Area: Treatment Point CV-24 or Under Lip*

  The conception vessel seems to be associated with emotions about one's sense of self. This encompasses shame, feelings of being undeserving, and/or not good enough.

Picture 10.3
Conception Vessel Focus Area

188

Below is a simple table (10.1) that you may use to help guide you in your self-testing. Begin by thinking about the problem you wish to treat, and then intuiting which emotion you might be feeling. Use your self-test to test the focus areas of the usual meridians that are associated with those emotions, and if you find that the focus area tests **yes** while you are thinking about the problem, you TAB on the meridian treatment point in the third column.

Table 10.1

Emotion	Self-Test	Treat
Anger	Heart	Little Finger
Pervasive Anger	Liver	Rib
Rage	Gall Bladder	Outside Eye
Trauma	Bladder	Inner Eye
Grief	Lungs	Thumb
Depression	Thyroid	Back of Hand
Anxiety	Stomach	Under Eye
Worry about future	Spleen	Under Arm
Fear	Kidney	Collarbone
Vulnerability	Small Intestine	Side of Hand
Guilt	Large Intestine	Index Finger
Shame	Central Vessel	Under Lip
Embarrassment	Governing Vessel	Under Nose
Jealousy	Circulation Sex	Middle Finger

Intuitive Knowing for Self-Treatment

Have you ever been trying to concentrate, particularly when you are very tired, and found yourself automatically putting your fingers on the bridge of your nose near your eyes? It is an automatic motion for many individuals and is very comforting. Interestingly, you were intuitively treating the bladder meridian pathway. Have you ever rested the sides of your fists on a table while trying to regain composure and found yourself more at ease? You were intuitively treating the small intestines meridian. There are many such examples when you have touched a meridian point intuitively and felt some comfort in the process.

Intuition as Your Guide

We stress that your intuition can be very valuable in helping you pick focus areas. Sometimes you may feel that a spot is itchy or pleasant and then you notice it is in the area of a focus area. Some people use the heart meridian as the site for love and forgiveness and will say positive affirmations while touching the treatment point for the heart meridian. In addition, you may find when you are taking a breath at a particular meridian point, that you just feel the need to stay there longer. We strongly encourage you to do so, taking as many breaths as you feel you need.

Self-Test for Treatment Points

When you decide that a particular focus area needs to be treated, you will use a self-test to check.

Examples

1. If you have no clues as to which treatment point requires your attention, you can go down the entire list of focus areas and self-test on each one. As you are thinking about your problem, you will get **yes** when you reach the one that needs treatment first.

2. You have an idea that the focus area is bladder because you wet the bed until you were three and were scolded for it. As you are

thinking about your problem, say to yourself, *"It is my bladder,"* and self-test. If you get **yes,** treat inner eye, the treatment point for bladder. If you get **no,** try another focus areas as you would in Step 1.

3. You have an idea that the focus area is stomach because it is the area associated with anxiety and you are feeling anxious. As you think about your problem, say to yourself, *"It is my stomach,"* and self-test. If you get **yes,** treat under eye, the treatment point for stomach. If you get **no,** try another focus area as you would in Step 1.

4. You have an idea that the focus area is kidney because you are having sensations in that area as you think about your problem. As you think about your problem, say to yourself, *"It is my kidney,"* and self-test. If you get **yes,** treat under the collarbone, the treatment point for kidney. If you get **no,** try another focus area as you would in Step 1.

5. You have an idea that the focus area is governing vessel for no reason except it popped into your mind when you looked at Picture 10.2. As you think about your problem, say to yourself, *"It is my governing vessel"* and self-test. If you get **yes** treat under nose, the treatment point for governing vessel. If you get **no,** try another focus area as you would in Step 1.

Strengthening Your Inner Communication

The benefit in using these techniques is that you may be strengthening your intuition not only as a guide to parts of yourself that need your attention; you may also be strengthening the inner communication between each cell in harmony with all your cells, all organs, and your total self.

Identifying Focus Areas in TAB

Now that you are aware of the different meridians and their corresponding emotions, you can use this knowledge to self-treat instead of using the full meridian treatment you learned in Chapter 4. While this may at first seem a bit more complicated, you can also go to www. energyofbelief.com to see a visual demonstration of what this treatment might entail.

Treatment Steps

Start by getting comfortable, drink some water and massage your neck and shoulders. If you feel disconnected or foggy, use a centering exercise from Chapter 7.

Step 1: Think About Your Problem (Attune Your Problem)

Pick a problem area, such as a disturbing memory, fear, behavior, belief, or thought on which you would like to work. Tune into one segment of the problem.

_____

_____

Step 2: Notice any Signs of Distress in Your Body

Focus your mind on the amount of distress the problem causes you in the present moment by scanning for any tension or disturbance in your body. If your problem has an element of enjoyment, focus your mind on the enjoyment and notice any areas of your body where you feel the enjoyment.

*My body sensations*_____

Step 3: Rate Your Distress with SUD and SUE Levels

SUD

Rate the amount of distress you are experiencing on a scale from 0 to ten where zero is no distress and ten is the worst you could experience. (Use the SUD scale in Chapter 2.)

My SUD level is _____

SUE

Rate the amount of enjoyment you are experiencing even though you know it is not good for you or causes grief for those you love on a scale from zero to ten, where zero is no enjoyment and 10 is the most enjoyment you could experience. (Use the SUE scale in Chapter 2). Remember what is important for SUE is the amount of enjoyment, even though it is not good for you or others.

My SUE level is _____

If you have both SUD and SUE levels work on the distress (SUD) first. When SUD is low, then work on the enjoyment (SUE).

Step 4: Rub the NLR and Make an Affirmation

Cross your hands over your chest and rub with deep pressure the area beneath your hands. You may find the spot a bit sore, which is normal. (Picture 10.4)

Make an affirmation three times.

Picture 10.4

Rubbing NLR

I accept myself even though I have (state your problem, fear, belief) _____

(its roots, causes, and all that it means and does to me and to others I love).

Step 5: State an Intention at the Side of Your Hand

State an intention for change as you touch the side of your hand and take one full respiration through your nose. (Picture 10.5)

Picture 10.5
Side of Hand

While touching the side of the hand meridian spot, state an intention. *I am ready/choosing to (be over this problem or release this problem)*_____
_____*(its roots, causes, and all it means and does to me and to others)*.

Repeat this three times.

Step 6: Think of Your Problem and Self-Test You Should Test No

(Note: when you think about your problem you should be **no** or **weak** before you start your work in TAB. If you test **yes,** go to Chapter 7 and check your polarity and neurological organization. If that is okay go to Chapter 8 and self-test for a blocking belief).

Step 7: Self-Test to Find a Focus Area

In order to find the first point, use your own inner signals and intuition. In addition you can use the list of emotions (List 10.1) and (Table 10.1) as guides. For example, when you think of the problem, you notice your stomach tighten; so you will self-test the stomach focus area first.

Step 8: Treat the Corresponding Meridian Treatment Point

When you test **yes** (strong or glide) on a focus point you should then TAB the corresponding meridian treatment point.

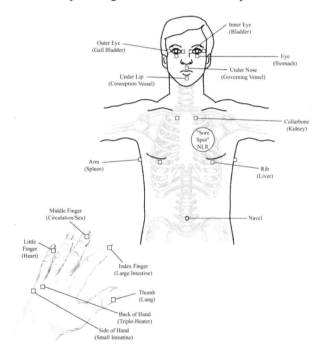

Illustration 10.1
TAB Treatment Point Locations

Step 9: Think of the Problem and Self-Test

After you've done TAB on a treatment point, think of the problem again. Self-test. If you are **no,** you must find another treatment point, so go back to Steps 7 and 8. You will go back to those two steps as many times as necessary.

Write down the points you treat because you will need to repeat them in Step 11. The number of points can be as few as one or as many as twenty or more. Points can repeat themselves but never in a row (i.e., you can get eye, arm, and collarbone but never eye, eye, collarbone).

When your self-test is **yes,** go to the next step.

Step 10: Do the Integration Sequence

Once you get a **yes** while thinking about the problem, it is a signal to do the integration sequence. Touch both collarbone treatment points at the same time using the tip of your thumb on one point and tips of your index, middle and ring fingers on the other point. With your other hand, use your index, middle and ring fingers to touch the back-of-hand treatment spot of the hand on your collarbone points.

Picture 10.6

Hand Position for Integration Sequence

1. Close eyes
2. Open eyes
3. Eyes look down to the right

4. Eyes look down to the left

5. Rotate the eyes in one full circle

6. Rotate the eyes in one full circle in the other direction

7. Hum a tune (for approximately five to seven seconds)

8. Count from one to five

9. Hum a tune again (for approximately five to seven seconds)

Step 11: Repeat the Treatment Sequence

Use all the points that were treated before the integration sequence. For example, if stomach and spleen were your focus areas and you treated under eye and under arm before the integration sequence, treat under eye and under arm again.

Step 12: Check Your Work-Rate — Your SUD and SUE Levels

Focus on your problem again.

Rate your distress on a scale from zero to ten. Did it get better, worse or stay the same? Rate your SUE level in the same way.

My SUD is _____ *My SUE is* _____

If your SUD and SUE are two or lower, go to Step 16, the eye-roll procedure. If your SUD and SUE are more than two, go to Step 13.

(Note: It is perfectly normal to change into a different and more intense thought or emotion. Just rub the NLR and state an accepting affirmation, return to Step 2 and begin to work on that problem.)

Step 13: Make an Affirmation Accepting That Your Self — Work is Incomplete

Rubbing the NLR spot (Picture 10.4), make your affirmation:

Affirmation formula: *I accept myself even though I am not **completely** over this problem (its roots, causes and all that it means to me and to others).*

Step 14: State an Intention for "Complete" Change

State an intention for "complete" change as you touch the side of your hand. (Picture 10.5)

I am ready/choosing to be **completely** *over* _____

_____

(its roots, causes, and all that it means to me and to others).

Step 15: Repeat the Process of Finding and Treating New Focus Areas

Go back to steps 6 through 11 and repeat the process of finding and treating a new treatment sequence by testing focus areas.

Continue to follow the instructions until your SUD is at a two or less. Then go to Step 16.

Step 16: End of Treatment Eye-Roll

When the SUD and SUE are two or less, use the eye-roll treatment. Touch both collarbone treatment points at the same time using the tip of your thumb on one point and tips of your index, middle and ring fingers on the other point. With your other hand, use your index, middle and ring fingers to touch the back of hand treatment spot of the hand on your collarbone points. (Picture 10.7)

Picture 10.7
Hand Position for Eye-Roll

While holding the points, take one full respiration drawing your mind energy to the points. Maintain contact with the collarbone points. Close your eyes. Open your eyes. Looking straight ahead, drop your eyes to the ground and slowly roll your eyes up to the sky taking five to seven seconds from ground to sky. At the top, relax back to a comfortable position.

Step 17: Check Your Work by Your SUD and SUE Levels

Check your work. SUD and SUE should be zero. If not go to Chapter 8 and see if there is a blocking belief impacting your success (i.e., it is not safe to be over this problem) and treat that belief.

My SUD level is _____ My SUE level is _____

Kasey's Treatment

Kasey is a single, 20-year-old woman who came into treatment after a severe car accident due to impaired judgment while she was driving under the influence of alcohol. Her drinking began in high school, escalated to the point where she couldn't function, and she had to drop out of college. As she reviewed her life story, she said that her life changed dramatically after a babysitter molested her when she was ten. Although she told her parents, who sought counseling for her, she just couldn't bring herself to talk about it, and completely shut down her feelings. "I just pretended all was Okay, did well in school and when I found alcohol, I felt much better inside because it really numbed my feelings."

Now, fresh out of rehab, she no longer wanted to use alcohol to numb her feeling and, determined to stay sober, she attended AA meetings; but the confusion and shame around the alcohol abuse was very intense. "When I think about alcohol my SUE level is a ten. I really want to drink."

Kasey decided to use the focus areas method of TAB on her drinking. She began by rubbing the NLR spot with an affirmation, "I accept myself even though I have a problem with drinking." She used TAB on the side of the hand with her intention, "I am choosing to reduce my urge to drink" and her self-test was strong. She rated the urge at a ten, and could feel tension in her head, shoulders, and hands. She tested her focus points.

As she tested these points she was surprised that her stomach and spleen (traditionally the first area affected by problems of anxiety) were not needed at that point. Then she tested gall bladder and it was **yes.** *She recognized this was rage and powerlessness; she admitted to herself, "I am angry." Kasey then used TAB on the gall bladder treatment points of her outer eyes. She thought about her urge, and tested weak. Continuing on to find the next focus area she tested* **yes** *to the liver, which is another anger point. Kasey treated the rib. When she thought about the problem, she tested* **yes,** *so she did the brain integration sequence, and then repeated the gall bladder and liver treatment points. Her SUE level went down to a five. She rubbed the NLR and made her affirmation, "I accept myself even though I am not completely free of this urge to drink" and she used TAB at the side of the hand, stating the intention, "I am ready to completely reduce my urge to drink." When she thought about the problem and self-tested she was* **no.** *She began to test other focus areas and got* **yes** *at the governing vessel and she also noticed a queasy feeling in her body, as if she wanted to throw up. She treated the governing vessel treatment point under her nose. She said, "I am embarrassed; I feel bad and ashamed about what happened to me as a child and also about my alcoholism." When she thought again about her problem, she was still* **no,** *so she tested her central vessel, because that focus area is associated with shame; she was* **yes,** *so she used TAB under her lip. Her self-test was weak, so she tried the spleen once again since she had this feeling that self-esteem and the future were still involved. This time the spleen area was* **yes,** *so she treated under her arm, the spleen point. Now when she self-tested thinking of the problem, she was* **yes.** *She did a brain integration sequence and repeated TAB on the governing vessel, central vessel, and spleen points.*

When she tested her SUE on drinking she was happy to report it was down to a two. She did an eye-roll. Her urge to drink was now zero.

Kasey was aware that this urge might return, and that now she had a technique to understand what emotions she was feeling, and a choice to use the technique rather than cover up the urge with alcohol. She felt empowered! Continued treatment with her therapist helped her to work on the molestation episode and eventually she was able to return to college and graduate.

It is very important to understand that for addictions it is necessary to use TAB (either with focus points or with the basic sequence) on a regular basis each time the urge occurs. The addiction, although problematic in and of itself, is usually an old solution to another problem. In our practices we have found that it takes at least several weeks of using TAB, each time an urge arises, to reduce the addictive desire on a permanent basis. It is also necessary to check for polarity and disorganization problems with addictions, because most people will have energetic disruptions when they come in contact with their substance (such as beer, chocolate, or cigarettes) and will not use TAB, even though they know it will help to reduce the urge. We see TAB as another tool that one can use to calm fears and anxieties rather than numbing out with the addiction.

Places for Personalized Work

You now have several opportunities to personalize your self-work. You can self-test to find whether your polarity is disorganized. You can also correct neurological disorganization should it come up during your work. You can notice when your treatments aren't effective, and then self-test to determine if there is a belief that is blocking you.

In addition, you now have several ways to find your own treatment points by noticing and intuiting. In following the fourteen-point method, if you sense that a particular point feels right, stay at that point for a few breaths, or as long as you would like. If a point pops into your mind, you can self-test to check whether the point should be used. You can check the meridian points to see what emotion corresponds with the point, and you can also use your emotions as a guide to treatment points. You can self-test to discover your own personal sequence if you wish. The more you explore your own intuitive sense of your energy needs, the more you open yourself to the opportunities for well-being.

Moving on to Chapter 11

You have now expanded the possibilities to use your intuition as a guide to increased self-awareness. Be curious and find what works best for you. In the next chapter you will learn how to practice and strengthen intention and use TAB coordinated with mindful practice to bring about a healthier future.

CHAPTER 11

Creating the Life You Want

Throughout this book you have learned to use TAB in response to a problem. Next we will explore how to be proactive with TAB, combining the energy of TAB with the energy of your imagination.

You have the inherent ability to imagine and rehearse a future event in your mind. You can imagine performing before you actually perform. Yet instead of using this gift to focus on what you would like in your life, most people spend a great deal of time imagining future catastrophes. If you can imagine the future you want with a clear intention, you will attract opportunities. In this chapter, you will learn how to use TAB strategies and sequences to imagine the successful completion of challenging activities, and achieve the behaviors you want.

Future Performance

The techniques of imagining future performance are not new to psychology. For decades, behaviorists and hypnotists have had patients imagine performing difficult behaviors or activities in order to overcome their fears. For example, imagining taking a long airplane flight for those who are afraid of flying, or imagining making a presentation for those with fear of public speaking, are common strategies.

Another use of imagining is for skills enhancement and is called peak performance coaching. The therapist coaches the patient in order to improve his or her ability to perform in such areas as sports, school, music, etc. Although imagining has been used for decades, including TAB to imagining future performance adds an energetic dimension. The images will be clearer and stronger in all your senses, and you will energetically resonate with the new behavior.

When to Use Future Performance in TAB

The future performance steps may be used after you have used TAB to work on a problem, and the SUD and SUE levels are at zero; or they may be used as stand-alone techniques. As an example of the former approach, Kasey, the college student we told you about in the last chapter who had an alcohol problem, used TAB to enhance her future behaviors after working on TAB to reduce her urge to drink. She used the future performance technique (described below) to help her to imagine being at a party with a diet soda in her hand, instead of a beer. She also imagined walking past her favorite bar without stopping and going to work out at the local gym instead. Using TAB helped strengthen her ability to imagine these behaviors and she reported it was much easier to do than she had expected.

At other times, you can use the future performance steps as a stand-alone technique to enhance performance. For example, you can imagine yourself going for a job interview, improving your golf swing, or doing well on an exam.

Imagining Future Performance for Success in the Present

We have found that some patients, with a history of physical or psychological trauma, have found future performance techniques extremely helpful at the beginning of their therapy. In spite of having a past filled with pain and suffering, most trauma survivors come to therapy for problems they are having currently at work, at school, or in a relationship. Often they are afraid that therapy will overwhelm them with memories or upsetting emotions before they are ready to deal with them. They want help for their present problem without having to deal with the pain of the past at the same time. Future performance techniques help them to focus on what they want in the present and for many, once they are able to have successful experiences with future performance techniques, and regain some control over the present problem, they feel more empowered and safe enough to work on the traumatic memories of the past.

Angela's Story

Angela is a quiet, unassuming woman in her mid-50s who, despite her fear of men, has managed to succeed in a high-powered public relations position. She reports that she grew up in a household where there was a great deal of violence. Her father was an alcoholic, and as a child, Angela was always on hyper-alert to be sure that she and her sisters would be ready for his outbursts, hoping to avoid his rages and beatings. When Angela first came to treatment, she did not want to revisit those days of abuse, but she did want to move forward with her life. She wanted to be less fearful of men, and hoped that TAB could help her without having to think about her past traumas. "If I could imagine myself grown up it would help," she said, "because there's a part of me that always feels very unsafe, like a little girl."

Despite her rise in the corporate world, she found that at every staff meeting whenever her boss raised his voice and questioned her work she immediately started to feel intense anxiety in her chest, and was unable to say anything intelligent. Angela was up for a promotion and there would be an important interview with her boss, her potential new boss, and the members of the new group she'd be joining. The group was all men and she was panicked. Her SUD was at a nine.

She tried to imagine herself sitting with relaxed shoulders, smiling, talking, and composed. Her SUFI level (subjective units of future imaging described below) was a one. She then rubbed the NLR and made her affirmation, "I accept myself even though I am unable to be calm in a meeting with my boss." She used TAB *at the side of hand and stated her intention, "I want to be able to know I am safe enough in the office." She then used TAB to reduce the distress associated with even thinking about the upcoming interview. It took several rounds of TAB, and she was able to imagine herself at a SUFI of seven. Although still cautious, she was much calmer. She was afraid to be any calmer, and didn't want to take it any further. A week later she reported the interview went **very** well, she was "calm enough," and gave intelligent answers to all the questions, even though her old boss asked challenging ones and even raised his voice. She got the promotion!*

SUFI (Subjective Units of Future Imagining) Scale: Zero to Ten Scale

You will be asking yourself, on a scale of zero to ten, how well can I imagine being successful in the future? On the SUFI scale, zero is "I cannot imagine myself having any success at all" and ten is "I can imagine myself completely successful in the future." Let's use the example of quitting smoking. A SUFI of zero would be, "I absolutely can't imagine myself not having a cigarette with my coffee," and a ten would be, "I can perfectly imagine myself drinking coffee without smoking." For peak sports performance in tennis, for example, a zero would be, "I cannot imagine myself staying focused when the official has miscalled the serve," and a ten would be, "I can imagine myself relaxed and concentrating on the next serve even though the official has miscalled the last one."

Future Performance Treatment Steps

The steps of future performance are similar to the steps you used in Chapter 5. This time you will be operating on your thought field from another perspective. Begin by getting comfortable, drinking water, and massaging your neck and shoulders. If you feel disconnected or foggy, use a centering exercise from Chapter 7. We especially recommend that you self-test for polarity and neurological disorganization when it is a peak performance issue such as a golf competition, or an upcoming important test.

Step 1: Select the Behavior You Would Like to Do

Select the behavior you want to have or the skill you would like to improve. Put it in as many words as needed, using as many senses as possible. For example, if it is going to be your first dinner party on your healthful eating project, you might say, "I want to enjoy the conversation at the dinner table. I want to chew my food slowly. I want to stop eating when I am full. I want to feel calm and free about my eating choices."

_____

_____

_____

Step 2: Notice any Signals in Your Body

Notice any areas of comfort or discomfort in your body when you think of it (i.e. smile, stomach tense, heart racing).

Areas of comfort or discomfort_____

Step 3: Rate Your Imagining with a SUFI Score

Get a SUFI scale score. Run through the behavior in your mind's eye, and then rate how clearly and comfortably you can imagine the behavior on a 0–10 scale. (Remember ten means "I am completely comfortable, and clear when I imagine myself doing this.") Notice how well you can imagine using all your senses: pictures, sounds, smells, tastes, touch, and intuition.

SUFI scale score _____

Step 4: Rub the NLR and Make an Affirmation

Picture 11.1
Rubbing the NLR

Cross your hands over your chest and rub with deep pressure on the area beneath your hands. You may find the spot a bit sore, which is normal.

Make an affirmation that sincerely acknowledges where you are now.

I accept myself even though I am unable to do this now (state specifically what you would like to do) _____

(Repeat this three times.)

Step 5: State an Intention at the Side of Your Hand

Touch the side of hand and mindfully state your intention: *I am ready/choosing to be able to do this.* _____

(State specifically what you wish to do here.)

Picture 11.2
Mindfully State Your Intention

Step 6: Mindfully Touch and Breathe
on Each of the Fourteen Meridian Points

Think about your problem. Touch each meridian treatment point and take a deep breath in and out at each point. You may take as many breaths as you like before moving on to the next point. Use Illustration 11.1 as your guide.

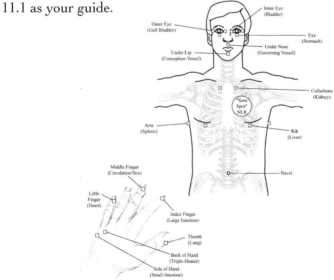

Illustration 11.1
TAB Treatment Point Locations

For the basic sequence, it is as follows:

1. Inner Eye
2. Outer Eye
3, Under Eye
4. Under Nose
5. Under Lip
6. Under Arm
7. Rib/Under Breast
8. Thumb
9. Index Finger
10. Middle Finger
11. Little Finger
12. Back of hand
13. Side of hand
14. Collarbone

Step 7: Do the Brain Integration Sequence

Touch both collarbone treatment points at the same time using the tip of your thumb on one point and tips of your index, middle and ring fingers on the other point. With your other hand, use your index, middle and ring fingers to touch the back-of-hand treatment spot of the hand on your collarbone points. (See Picture 11.3)

Picture 11.3

Hand Position for Integration Sequence

1. Close eyes

2. Open eyes

3. Eyes look down to the right

4. Eyes look down to the left

5. Rotate the eyes in one full circle

6. Rotate the eyes in one full circle in the other direction

7. Hum a tune (for approximately five to seven seconds)

8. Count from one to five

9. Hum a tune again (for approximately five to seven seconds)

Step 8: Repeat the Treatment Sequence

Touch each of the fourteen meridian treatment points again, taking as many deep breaths at each point as you feel you need.

Step 9: Check Your Work — Rate Your SUFI

Focus on your desired behavior again.

My SUFI level is _____

If your SUFI level is an eight or higher, go to Step 16 and do an eye-roll.

If your SUFI level is less than eight, go to Step 10.

Step 10: Rub the NLR and Make an Affirmation Accepting That Your Self-Work is Incomplete

Affirmation formula: *I accept myself even though I am not **completely** able to imagine doing this new behavior* _____

(State the behavior you wish to address.)

Step 11: State an Intention for "Complete" Change

State an intention for "complete" change as you TAB the side of your hand:

*I am ready/choosing to be **completely** able to* _____

_____

Step 12: Mindfully Touch and Breathe on Each of the Fourteen Points

Step 13: Do the Brain Integration Sequence

Step 14: Repeat the Treatment Sequence

Step 15: Check Your SUFI Level

If the SUFI level is eight or higher, go to Step 16. If less than eight, go back to Step 10 and repeat Steps 10 to 15. You may do this as many times as necessary, but it may be better after three tries to self-test for blocking beliefs, and work on those.

Step 16: End of Treatment Eye-Roll

Touch both collarbone treatment points at the same time using the tip of your thumb on one point and tips of your index, middle and ring fingers on the other point. With your other hand, use your index, middle and ring fingers to touch the back of hand treatment spot of the hand on your collarbone points. (See Picture 11.4)

Picture 11.4
Hand Position for Eye-Roll

While holding the points, take one full respiration while drawing your mind energy to the points. Maintain contact with the collarbone points. Close your eyes. Open your eyes. Looking straight ahead, drop your eyes to the ground and slowly roll your eyes up to the sky taking five to seven seconds to look from the ground to the sky. At the top, relax back to a comfortable position.

Step 17: Check Your Work by Imagining the New Behavior and Taking a SUFI level

My SUFI level is _____

Mindful Practice Makes Perfect

In the 1970s, radio research scientist R. H. Barfield wrote, "The material world is precipitated from a nonmaterial world: from a world of *thought*, which is an ultimate reality...." (Barfield, 1976, p. 81) Barfield goes on to say that thought is as familiar to us as breath, so we tend to take it for granted and ignore its possibilities for the material world. It is now time for you to use your thoughts to create the reality of positive options in your future. It is time to practice being in the future — doing what it is you want to do, being how you want to be and actually experiencing your intention. Imagining can create a new ending to a tragedy, or provide an opportunity for rehearsal either to overcome a bad habit or improve one's skills for peak performance.

A New Ending to a Tragedy

Like many people who have lost a loved one, Frank (Chapter 8) and Peter (Chapter 9) had the belief that they would lose their connection to their loved one if they let go of the grief or the traumatic images. They first used TAB to release the negative images and beliefs surrounding the deaths and then used TAB to develop a positive emotional connection to their loved ones. Below is an example of the technique used for both Peter and Frank to imagine a rainbow image connecting them energetically to their loved ones.

Peter's Treatment Continued

Peter used TAB to decrease his SUD level to a zero when thinking about the traumatic images of his son's car accident. Then, Peter imagined John was standing in front of him in the room.

First, Peter imagined speaking to his son from his heart, saying that he was sorry that John was so stuck in the gambling, and that he, Peter, was unable to help him. He then imagined what John might say in return, and found himself thinking that John wanted to apologize too, for being so difficult. Peter then imagined a rainbow from his heart to John's heart and imagined love pulsing between them both. His SUFI score was a three when he began, but he rubbed his NLR and affirmed, "I accept myself even though this is hard to imagine"; he then used TAB at the side of hand and stated, "I am choosing to imagine this connection to my son." He used TAB on all the meridian points, did the brain integration sequence and then TAB on all the points. His SUFI score then went to an eight. He used an eye-roll, and reported he could actually feel the love between them. He wiped tears from his eyes and stated his new belief was, "Love never dies."

Overcoming a Bad Habit

Etienne's story demonstrates one of the many ways that you can use TAB to create a new script for yourself when an old script is robbing you of your options.

Etienne's Story

Some thiry pounds over the weight the doctor had said would be healthy for him, Etienne, a 37-year-old attorney, had a self-described "eating addiction." He said he wouldn't eat during the day and looked forward to dinner with his wife and children when he'd get home around seven in the evening. He reported that he enjoyed the dinner, but it was always over too fast; his wife and the kids ate quickly and then got up leaving him alone at the table. He wanted everyone to slow down and talk. After they were gone, he would continue to eat from the serving dishes and whatever was left on the children's plates. Then he'd help his wife clean up by bringing the emptied plates to the sink. After dinner, he would feel empty and would then rummage through the refrigerator and eat nonstop until he went to bed at midnight. He stated he just couldn't imagine not doing that; it had become an "automatic" routine.

Etienne spent his early life in an orphanage and was adopted by his American parents at the age of six. As a child he was emaciated and his adoptive parents, who were very overweight, plied him with concern and food. They were very loving and he always associated eating with their love. He soon put on extra pounds and had never been concerned about his weight gain until his doctor told him that his cholesterol was dangerously high and that his heart was showing early signs of heart disease. Though he knew he had to lose weight, Etienne was frightened at the thought of doing so. He knew that his fear was due to the deprivation he had experienced during childhood, yet he was unwilling to discuss his early childhood.

Etienne started his treatment by imagining himself getting up from the table when his wife got up, placing his both hands on a plate and bringing it to the sink. He then imagined kissing his wife and going up to change into a sweatsuit in order to take a walk with her. His wife agreed that the dishes could be left in the sink while they walked. He then imagined talking to her while she began washing the dishes he'd brought to the sink. He found that while talking to her, he could return to the table and bring back more dishes without eating from them. He also *imagined that he could ask the children to help by taking the dishes to the sink as well. At first, he could hardly picture it because as he put it, "it would be so different!" His SUFI was at a three. He used the future techniques, and his imaging was now a seven. Excited, he did TAB saying, "I am ready to **completely** be able to do this," and he did another round of TAB. When he pictured this new behavior it was a ten, and when he tried to imagine the old behavior of going to the refrigerator and eating, he was unable to do so because the new image was stronger.*

Better Performance

Whether you want to improve in a sport or do better in school, imagining yourself in the future is useful. It is best to consider if there were any past events that would interfere with your imagining the future with comfort and clearing out any prior difficulties.

Don's Story

Future performance techniques are extremely powerful in improving your performance in sports. In addition, it is also helpful to use the techniques in Chapter 7 because, if your timing is off even slightly in sports such as tennis or golf, the results can be disastrous.

Don was a 17-year old teenager who had been playing golf since age four and won his first junior league tournament at age five. As he entered his teens he told his therapist that if left to his own choices, he would happily play golf all day long with friends, but tournaments had become another story. Once his reputation for being a good teen golfer got around, he had begun to feel a pressure to win, and what had previously been just a fun sport had become competitive and stressful. "All the fun has gone out of it."

Don was not aware that when he was laughing and having fun, his system was neurologically organized and positive so he was a "natural" winner. However when he was competing, his system frequently became disorganized and as a result his performance was inconsistent. Like most athletes, he was willing to do anything to improve his game so he practiced visualizing himself winning the matches, and did the centering exercises before playing the next important match, plus one round of TAB, just to be sure he was in a peak state. During that match he could be seen swinging his arms from side to side, moving his eyes in a figure of eight pattern, discreetly holding under his arm, under his eye and his side of hand spot, while taking a deep breath. No one, except his parents, knew what he was up to.

Not only did he win but, more importantly, his enjoyment of the game returned!

Clara's Story

School is another area when using these methods can enhance your ability to take tests, give a speech to the class, and to generally perform at your peak.

Clara is a charming 17-year-old high school student with dreams of going to a good college. Throughout high school she did well on her papers and short quizzes; however, she struggled with tests, especially the standardized type. "I just freeze up and forget everything I know." She took testing classes and used the strategies that testing centers recommended. She took the practice exams over and over, yet her scores remained too low to be accepted into the school she wanted. She came into counseling for help with the upcoming SAT.

In her therapy session, Clara first used TAB to work on the negative belief that had built up that told her she would never be able to do well on tests. She also learned how fix her polarity and neurological disorganization. Using the future protocol she pictured herself taking the SAT exam, feeling comfortable when faced with a difficult question, and finishing with enough time to check her answers. She did several rounds of TAB on each of these images until they were strong. The morning of the exam she used all the strategies before she left her house, and reported that during the exam she was so calm and in such a peak state that she didn't even need to do a treatment. At her break she did the treatment sequence again, although she stated she didn't even think she needed to do them. She was so happy and grateful to have mastered these methods, and her score said it all; they represented the excellent student she truly was. Her score was over 170 points higher than any previous test score and she was now able to apply to the school she desired, plus she was no longer fearful of taking tests.

There is no limit to the many areas in which you can use future imagining techniques to improve your life. From test-taking, to sports, to public speaking, and to job interviews, the list is endless; if you can imagine it, you can do it and be it. If you can see it, hear it, feel it, taste it, smell it, intend it and organize your energy, by the very laws of the universe you will resonate with the situation and make it happen. Do not let any of your fears, old triggers or negative beliefs, stop you. Focus your energy, state your intention, remove any blocking beliefs and you are there!

Moving on to Chapter 12

In the next chapter you will learn more about what we mean by resonating with the energy of others and the energy of the world. You will learn that centering and letting go of limiting beliefs as an individual has a much larger effect on your life and the world around you than you may have ever imagined possible.

CHAPTER 12

World Peace Begins
with Inner Peace

Although this is the last chapter of our book, we intend for it to be the beginning of new ways to view your life; and also your impact on those around you, not only on the small circle of your intimate world, but to the larger circle that expands out into the world. In this last chapter we will explore how your healing is connected to world healing and your progress is linked to world progress. We propose that, as you create your own inner peace and allow yourself to be open to healthier and kinder options in your life; you promote an expansion of the same peacefulness and kindness in the world as a whole.

Sheila Writes

There is a need for research studies that take a fresh perspective to investigate the power of TAB and the influence you as an individual could exert in the greater society through your own mind's work. How could such studies be developed? Cognitive scientist, Douglas Hofstadter (1981, p. 458) expressed this beautifully: "Coming to understand the mind will probably require new ways of thinking that are at least as outrageous at first as Copernicus's shocking suggestion that the Earth goes around the Sun, or Einsteins's bizarre claim that space itself could be curved. Science advances haltingly, bumping against the boundaries of the unthinkable: the things declared impossible because they are currently unimaginable. It is at the speculative frontier of thought experiment and fantasy that these boundaries get adjusted." In the new millennium the boundaries of the mind are definitely being pushed with concepts from physics like zero-point fields. Lynne McTaggert (2002, 2007) and Bernard Haisch (2006) have written in depth on the topic. For the purpose of this book, you need only know that what seems to be empty space in the universe is in actuality the place in which energy flows together in perfect balance. Such a place could provide the hypothetical constructs required to explain the speed of thought and the location of the thought fields that bind them. Zero-point fields could provide us with one way to understand the connectedness of your thoughts to the universe, your mind, and the effects of TAB.

In this time of exciting possibilities, we are setting our intention that TAB will be used throughout the world to empower people to heal and be at peace, and that researchers will come forward to help us understand the mechanisms of its effectiveness.

Mary Writes

As a clinician, I repeatedly found that as my clients used these methods and began to feel more and more in control of their emotions and beliefs, an added benefit was that they became more peaceful and loving. It was as if instead of being "contracted" with their fears, self-defeating beliefs or behaviors that they were ashamed of, they were now able to feel more expansive, loving, and generous toward others. Unburdened by the fears and guilt that held them back, they naturally moved into a more peaceful state, and were then were able to extend that peace more easily throughout their families, communities, and the world. It was not unusual to hear family members commenting on these changes also.

I began to wonder, what is happening here? As I searched for answers, I came to believe that as you use these methods on your own fears and negative self-beliefs, you will naturally return to the wholeness of who you really are. You will no longer feel as competitive toward others, as you recognize your own power to create and achieve what you desire. I found that for myself and clients, using these methods repeatedly, your heart expands and you become less angry and judgmental of yourself and others. You recognize that you are no longer a victim of your painful experiences and beliefs; you are now able to neutralize them so that you are not always triggered into the past. You are able to live more and more in the present moment, or be "in the now" that many spiritual teachers speak about.

Spiritual masters of all religions teach that divinity resides within us, and that we cannot be separated from it. When our fears and beliefs block us from remembering our true essence, we feel lost and disconnected from our Source, and inner peace eludes us. It is from this position of doubt and fear, that we create division and war.

I invite you to seriously consider using the techniques in this book each and every time you act, think, or feel in a way that you do not like. Use TAB when you are feeling irritated waiting for the repair man, or when those automatic, negative judgments pop into your head as you listen to someone whose view is different from your own. Most importantly, recognize the power of your "I am" statements and each time you find yourself making a negative "I am" statement, stop and use TAB on the origin of that belief. I invite you to look at the pervasive self-defeating beliefs that seem to run your life, and use the techniques we've taught you to create healthier beliefs for yourself. I also encourage you to imagine yourself achieving all of your dreams. The more you use these techniques to calm and center yourself and release those blocking beliefs, the more you will transform your life and find that elusive "inner peace" that we are all longing for. Without fear, you will automatically strengthen your connection to Source. As more and more of us work to create inner peace, we contribute to the real possibility of world peace. How blessed would this world be if each of us would do our part.

Wrapping Up and Moving Forward

In the first chapter we described the philosophy in the 1960s, which foretold that we humans were doomed because of our brain deficits. Hopefully, your self-work with TAB has given you renewed optimism that you, as part of the human race, can build energetic connections that enable you to be less reactive, that allow you to think through problems and then make a choice as to what actions to take. We truly hope that, through learning the Touch and Breathe techniques, we have given you the inspiration for moving forward.

Bibliography

Averill, J. R. and More, T. A. (2004). "Happiness." In M. Lewis and J.M.Haviland-Jones (Eds.), *Handbook of Emotions* (second edition pp. 663–676). New York: Guilford Press.

Barfield, R. H. (1976). "Darwinism." In S. Sugarman (Ed.), *Evolution of Consciousness: Studies in Polarity* (pp. 69–82). CT: Wesleyan University Press.

Becker, R. O., and Seldon, G. (1985). *The Body Electric.* New York: Morrow.

Becker, R. O. (1990). *Cross Currents: The Perils of Electropollution, the Promise of Electromedicine.* New York: Putnam.

Bender, S. S., Lange, G., Steffener, J., Bergmann, U., Grand, D., Liu, W., Bly, B. M. (2000). "Imaging violence: Post-traumatic stress disorder, eye movement desensitization and reprocessing, and functional magnetic resonance imaging." (This study was supported by seed grant funds from the Violence Institute of New Jersey — Index #103772). UMDNJ-Newark.

Bernstein, J. (1991). *Quantum Profiles.* Princeton, NJ: Princeton University Press.

Blaich, R. M. (1988, winter). Applied kinesiology and human performance. *Collected Papers of International College of Applied Kinesiology* (pp. 7–15). Shawnee Mission, KS: International College of Applied Kinesiology.

Bohm, D. (1976). "Imagination, fancy, insight and reason in the process of thought." In S. Sugarman (Ed.), *Evolution of Consciousness: Studies in Polarity* (pp. 51–68). CT: Wesleyan University Press.

Bohm, D., and Hiley, B. (1993). *The Undivided Universe: An Ontological Interpretation of Quantum Theory.* New York: Routledge.

Burr, H. S. (2004). *Blueprint for Immortality.* England: CW Daniel Company.

Callahan, R. J. (1981, winter). "Psychological reversal." *Collected Papers of the International College of Applied Kinesiology* (pp. 79–96). Shawnee Mission, KS: International College of Applied Kinesiology

Callahan, R. J. (1985). *Five-Minute Phobia Cure.* Wilmington, DE: Enterprise.

Callahan, R. J. (with P. Perry) (1991). *Why Do I Eat When I'm Not Hungry?* New York: Doubleday.

Callahan, R. J. (1992). *Special Report #1: The Cause of Psychological Problems: Introduction to Theory.* Indian Wells, CA: Author.

Callahan, R. J. and Callahan, J. (1996). *Thought Field Therapy and Trauma: Treatment and Theory.* Indian Wells, CA: Authors.

Childre, D., Martin, H., and Beech, D. (1999). *The Heart/Math Solution.* San Francisco: HarperCollins.

Church, D. (2007). *The Genie in Your Genes: Epigenetic Medicine and the New Biology of Intention.* CA: Elite Books.

Conable, K. M. and Hanicke, B. T., (1987). Inter-examiner agreement in applied kinesiology manual muscle testing. *Selected Papers of the International College of Applied Kinesiology.* Shawnee Mission, KS: ICAK.

Connolly, S. (2004). *Thought Field Therapy: Clinical Applications — Integrating TFT in Psychotherapy.* AZ: George Tyrell Press — available through www. thoughtfieldtherapy.net/

Craig, G. and Fowlie, A. (1997). *Emotional Freedom Techniques: The Manual.* The Sea Ranch, CA: Author.

Dalai Lama (1999). *The Art of Happiness.* NY: Riverhead Books.

Davies, P. C. W., and Brown, J. R. (1986). *The Ghost in the Atom.* Cambridge: Cambridge University Press.

Dennison, P., and Dennison, P. (1994). *Brain Gym.* Ventura, CA: Edu-Kinesthetics.

Diamond, J. (1985). *Life Energy: Using the Meridians to Unlock the Hidden Power of Your Emotions.* NY: Paragon House.

Diepold, J. H. Jr. (1998). "Touch and Breathe (TAB): An Alternative Treatment Approach with Meridian-Based Psychotherapies." Paper presented at Innovative and Integrative Approaches to Psychotherapy: A Conference. Edison, NJ.

Diepold, J. H. Jr. (2000). "Touch and Breathe (TAB): An Alternative Treatment Approach with Meridian-Based Psychotherapies." *Electronic Journal of Traumatology*, 6 (2). Available: http://www.fsu.edu/~trauma/v6i2/contv6i2.html

Diepold, J. H. Jr. (2002). "Thought Field Therapy: Advancements in Theory and Practice." In F. Gallo (Ed.), *Energy Psychology in Psychotherapy* (pp. 3–34). New York: W.W. Norton.

Diepold, J., Britt, V., and Bender, S. (2004). *Evolving Thought Field Therapy: The Clinician's Handbook of Diagnoses, Treatment, and Theory.* New York: W. W. Norton.

Durlacher, J. (1995). *Freedom from Fear Forever.* Van Ness.

Eden, D. and Feinstein, D. (1998). *Energy Medicine.* New York: Jeremy P. Tarcher/Putnam.

Eddington, A. (1958). *The Philosophy of Physical Science.* The University of Michigan Press: Ann Arbor Paperbacks.

Field, T. (2001). *Touch.* Cambridge: The MIT Press.

Figley, C. R. and Carbonell, J. (1995). The "Active Ingredient" Project: the systematic clinical demonstration of the most efficient treatments of PTSD, a research plan. Tallahassee: Florida State University Psychosocial Stress Research Program and Clinical Laboratory.

First International Fascia Research Congress (October 2007). Harvard Medical School, Boston.

Fleming, T. (1996). *Reduce Traumatic Stress in Minutes: The Tapas Acupressure Technique (TAT) Workbook.* Torrance, CA: Tapas Fleming.

Feinstein, D., Eden, D. and Craig, G. (2005). *The Promise of Energy Psychology: Revolutionary Tools for Dramatic Personal Change.* New York: Tarcher/Penguin.

Furman, M. E. (2002). "Grounding Energy Psychology in the Physical Sciences." In F. Gallo (Ed.), *Energy Psychology in Psychotherapy* (pp. 368–386). New York: W.W. Norton.

Gallo, F. (2000). *Energy Psychology: Explorations at the Interface of Energy, Cognition, Behaviors, and Health.* Boca Raton: CRC Press.

Gallo, F., Ed. (2002). *Energy Psychology in Psychotherapy: A Comprehensive Source Book.* New York: W.W. Norton.

Gallo, F. (2007). *Energy Tapping for Trauma: Rapid Relief from Post-Traumatic Stress Using Energy Psychology.* Oakland, CA: New Harbinger Publications.

Gendlin, E. T. (1996). "The Use of Focusing in Therapy." In J. K. Zeig (ed.), *The Evolution of Psychotherapy*, (p. 197–210). New York: Brunner/Mazel.

Gerber, R. (1988). *Vibrational Medicine: New Choices for Healing Ourselves.* Santa Fe, NM: Bear.

Gillispie, C. C. (1960). *The Edge of Objectivity: An Essay in the History of Scientific Ideas.* New Jersey: Princeton University Press.

Greenfield, S. (2000). *The Private Life of the Brain: Emotions, Consciousness and the Secret of the Self.* New York: John Wiley and Sons, Inc.

Haisch, B. (2006). *The God Theory: Universes, Zero-Point Fields and What's Behind it All.* San Francisco, CA: Weiser Books.

Hofstadter, D., and Dennett, D., Eds. (1981). *The Mind's I: Fantasies and Reflections on Self and Soul.* New York: Basic Books, Inc.

Kabat-Zinn, J. (2005). *Coming to our Senses: Healing Ourselves and the World Through Mindfulness.* New York: Hyperion.

Kandel, E. R. (2007). *In Search of Memory: The Emergence of a New Science of Mind.* New York: W. W. Norton.

Kaptchuck, T. J., (1983). *The Web That Has No Weaver.* New York: Congdon and Weed.

Kendall, H. O. and Kendall, F. M. P. (1949). *Muscles: Testing and Function.* Baltimore: Williams and Wilkins.

Koestler, A. (1967). *The Ghost in the Machine: The Urge to Self Destruction: A Psychological and Evolutionary Study of Modern Man's Predicament.* New York: The MacMillan Company.

Konner, M. (1982). *The Tangled Wing: Biological Constraints on the Human Spirit.* New York: Holt, Rinehart and Winston.

Kuhn, T. S. (1964). "A Function for Thought Experiments." In A. Koyre (Ed.), *Histoire de la Pense: L'aventure de L'esprit.* Paris: Herman.

Kuhn, T. S. (1996). *The Structure of Scientific Revolutions,* third edition. Chicago and London: The University of Chicago Press.

Lambrou, P. and Pratt, G. (2000). *Instant Emotional Healing.* New York: Broadway Books.

Levine, Peter. (1997). *Waking the Tiger: The Innate Capacity to Transform Overwhelming Experiences.* CA: North Atlantic Books.

Lewis, M., and Haviland-Jones, J. M., (Eds.) (2004, second edition). *Handbook of Emotions.* New York: Guilford Press.

Lipton, B. (2005). *The Biology of Belief: Unleashing the Power of Consciousness, Matter and Miracles.* CA: Mountain of Love/Elite Books.

McTaggert, L. (2002). *The Field: The Quest for the Secret Force of the Universe.* New York: HarperCollins.

Mercola, J. and Ball, R. (2006). *Freedom at Your Fingertips: Get Rapid Physical and Emotional Relief with the Breakthrough System of Tapping.* Fredericksburg, VA: Inroads Publishing.

Monti, D. A., Sinnott, J., Marchese, M., Kunkel, E. J. S. and Greeson, J. M. (1999). "Muscle Test Comparisons of Congruent and Incongruent Self-Referential Statements." *Perceptual and Motor Skills.* 1019–1028.

Morowitz, H. J. (1981). "Rediscovering the Mind." In D. Hofstadter and D. Dennett (Eds.), *The Mind's I: Fantasies and Reflections on Self and Soul* (pp. 34–49). New York: Basic Books, Inc.

Nambudripad, D. (1993). *Say Goodbye to Illness.* Buena Park, CA: Delta Publishing.

Naparstek, B. (1998). *Your Sixth Sense: Unlock the Power of Your Intuition.* New York: Harper One.

Naparstek, B. (2004) *Invisible Heroes: Survivors of Trauma and How They Heal.* New York: Bantam Dell.

Nims, L. (2001). *BSFF Training Manual: Behavioral and Emotional System Elimination Training for Resolving Excess Emotion, Fear, Anger, Sadness, Trauma.* Orange, CA: Author.

Ornish, D. (1999). *Love and Survival: The Scientific Basis for the Healing Power of Intimacy.* New York: Collins.

Oschman, J. L. (2000). *Energy Medicine: The Scientific Basis.* Leith Walk, Edinburgh, UK: Churchill Livingstone/Harcourt Publishers Limited.

Pearsall, P. (1998). *The Heart's Code.* New York: Random House.

Penfield, W. (1969). "Conciousness, Memory, and Man's Conditioned Reflexes." In K.H. Pribram (Ed.), *On the Biology of Learning* (pp. 127–168). New York: Harcourt, Brace.

Pert, C. (1997). *Molecules of Emotion: The Science Behind Mind-Body Medicine.* NewYork: Scribner.

Rapp, D. (2004). *Our Toxic World: A Wake-up Call.* Buffalo, NY: Environmental Medical Research Foundation.

Restak, R. (2003). *The New Brain: How the Modern Age is Rewiring Your Mind.* USA: Rodale.

Rose, S. (2005). *The Future of the Brain: The Promise and Perils of Tomorrow's Neuro-science.* New York: Oxford University Press.

Rosenthal-Schneider, I. (1980). *Reality and Scientific Truth: Discussions with Einstein, von Laue, and Planck.* Detroit, Michigan: Wayne State University Press.

Sai Maa Lakshmi Devi. (2006). *Petals of Grace.* Crestone, CO: HIU Press.

Scaer, R. (2007). *The Body Bears the Burden: Trauma, Dissociation and Disease.* Binghampton, NY: Haworth Medical Press.

Schwartz, G. E., and Russek, G. (1997). Dynamical energy systems and modern physics: Fostering the science and spirit of complementary and alternative medicine. *Alternative Therapies,* 3(3), pp. 46–56.

Schwartz, J. M., and Begley, S. (2002). *The Mind and the Brain: Neuroplasticity and the Power of Mental Force.* New York: HarperCollins Publishers, Inc.

Scott, S. H. (2006). "Neuroscience: Converting Thoughts into Action." *Nature,* 442, pp. 164–171.

Servan-Schreiber, D. (2003). *The Instinct to Heal: Curing Stress, Anxiety, and Depression Without Drugs and Without Talk Therapy.* USA: Rodale, Inc.

Sheldrake, R. (1995). *The Presence of the Past: Morphic Resonance and the Habits of Nature.* Rochester, VT: Park Street.

Sheely, N., and Church, D. (2006). *Soul Medicine: Awakening Your Inner Blueprint for Abundant Health and Energy.* CA: Elite Books.

Thich, N. H. (1999). *The Miracle of Mindfulness.* MA: Beacon Press.

Tiller, W. A. (1997). *Science and Human Transformation: Subtle Energies, Intentionality and Consciousness.* Walnut Creek, CA: Pavior.

Tiller, W. A. (2001). *Conscious Acts of Creation: The Emergence of a New Physics.* CA: Pavior.

van der Kolk, B. A. (1994). "The Body Keeps the Score: Memory and the Evolving Psychobiology of Post-Traumatic Stress." *Harvard Review Psychiatry,* 1, pp. 253–265.

van der Kolk, B. A., McFarlane, A. C., and Weisaeth, L. (Eds.) (1996). *Traumatic Stress: The Effects of Overwhelming Experience on Mind, Body, and Society.* New York: Guilford.

Voll, R. (1975). "Twenty Years of Electro Acupuncture Diagnosis in Germany: A Progress Report." *American Journal of Acupuncture,* 3, pp. 7–17.

Walther, D. S. (1981). *Applied kinesiology: Vol. 1. Basic Procedures and Muscle Testing.* Pueblo, CO: Systems DC.

Walther, D. S. (1988). *Applied Kinesiology: Synopsis.* Pueblo, CO: Systems DC.

Wells, S., Polglase, K. A., Andrews, H. B. and Carrington, P. (2000). "A Meridian-Based Intervention (EFT) vs. Diaphragmatic Breathing in the Treatment of Specific Phobias." http://www.eftsupport.com/research_eft.htm

Whisenant, W. F. (1994). *Psychological Kinesiology: Changing the Body's Beliefs.* Kailua, HI: Monarch Butterfly Press.

White, Geoffrey M. (2004). "Representing Emotional Meaning: Category, Metaphor, Schema, Discourse." In M. Lewis and J. M. Haviland-Jones (Eds.), *Handbook of Emotions* (second edition, pp. 30–34). New York: Guilford Press.

Wolpe, J. and Lazarus, A. (1966). *Behavior Therapy and Beyond: A Guide to the Treatment of Neuroses.* London: Pergamon Press.

Woollerton, H., and McLean, C. J. (1986). *Acupuncture Energy in Health and Disease.* Wellingsborough, Northhamptonshire: Thorsons Publishers.

Worsley, J. R. (1993). *Traditional Chinese Acupuncture: Meridians and Points.* Boston: Element Books, Inc.

Related Literature

Arenson, G. (2001). *Five Simple Steps to Emotional Healing.* New York: Simon and Schuster.

Benor, D. (2006). *Personal Spirituality.* Bellmawr, NJ: Wholistic Healing Publications.

Benor, D. (2004). *Consciousness, Bioenergy and Healing: Self-Healing and Energy Medicine for the 21st Century.* (Healing Research, Vol. 2; Professional Edition). Bellmawr, NJ: Wholistic Healing Publications.

Borysenko, J. and Dveirin, G. (2007). *Your Soul's Compass: What is Inner Guidance?* Carlsbad, CA: Hay House.

Damasio, A. (2003). *Looking for Spinoza: Joy, Sorrow and the Feeling Brain.* Orlando, FL: Harcourt, Inc.

Dyer, W. (2004). *The Power of Intention.* CA: Hay House.

Hartung, J. and Galvin, M. (2003). *Energy Psychology and EMDR: Combining Forces to Optimize Treatment.* New York: W.W. Norton.

Hover-Kramer, D. (2002). *Creative Energies: Psychology for Self-Expression and Healing.* New York: W. W. Norton.

Hover-Kramer, D. and Shames, K. H. (1997). *Energetic Approaches to Emotional Healing.* New York: Delmar Publishers.

Phillips, M., PhD. (2000). *Finding the Energy to Heal: How EMDR, Hypnosis, TFT, Imagery, and Body-Focused Therapy Can Help Restore Mindbody Health.* New York: W. W. Norton.

Tucker, J. (2000). *Insight Inspirations: Messages of Hope.* Middletown, MD: Inner Change Consulting

Website Resources for Finding Energy Practitioners

ACEP: Association for Comprehensive Energy Psychology.
www.energypsych.org/

Daniel Benor, MD. www.WholisticHealingResearch.com

Be Set Free Fast (Larry Nims). www.bsff.org

Energy Medicine: (Eden, Donna). www.Innersource.net

EFT: (Gary Craig). www.emofree.com

Evolving Thought Field (EvTFT): (John Diepold, Victoria Britt, Sheila
Bender). www.tftworldwide.com

Foundation for Energy and Spiritual Healing: (Phil Friedman).
www.philipfriedman.com/

Healing from the Body Level Up: (Judith Swack). www.jaswack.com

Allergy Antidotes: (Sandra Radomski). www.allergyantidotes.com.

Seemorg Matrix: (Asha Clinton). www.seemorgmatrix.com

TAT: Tapas Acupressure Technique: (Tapas Fleming). www.tatlife.net

Thought Field Therapy: Callahan Techniques (Roger Callahan).
www.tftrx.com

Traditional Chinese Medicine World Foundation (Nan Lu).
www.tcmconference.org

Index